Sarah L. Larimer

The Capture and Escape; or, Life Among the Sioux

Sarah L. Larimer

The Capture and Escape; or, Life Among the Sioux

ISBN/EAN: 9783337055769

Printed in Europe, USA, Canada, Australia, Japan

Cover: Foto ©ninafisch / pixelio.de

More available books at **www.hansebooks.com**

THE CAPTURE AND ESCAPE;

OR,

LIFE AMONG THE SIOUX.

.BY

Mrs. SARAH L. LARIMER.

I beheld the westward marchers
Of the unknown crowded nations.
All the road was full of people,
Restless, struggling, toiling, striving.
LONGFELLOW.

PHILADELPHIA:

CLAXTON, REMSEN & HAFFELFINGER,

819 & 821 MARKET STREET.

1871.

TO

The People of the West,

THIS NARRATIVE IS INSCRIBED BY ONE WHO

COUNTS MANY FRIENDS AMONG THEM,

AND CLAIMS A HOME IN THEIR

PROSPEROUS LAND.

S. L. L.

PREFACE.

MORE than five years have elapsed since the great Indian War of the plains commenced, by the raid of a band of roving, hostile Indians upon a small company of emigrants that were en route to the gold regions of Idaho.

The attack was at Little Box-Elder Creek, in Idaho Territory. I was of that unfortunate company; and, after this interval, which has brought desolation and death among the frontier people, I have endeavored to narrate briefly my experience with the Indians, and to record some observations of Indian life and character.

CONTENTS.

CHAPTER I.

CHAPTER II.

CHAPTER III.

CHAPTER IV.

CHAPTER V.

CHAPTER VI.

CHAPTER VII.

CHAPTER VIII.

CHAPTER IX.

CHAPTER X.

CHAPTER XI.

CHAPTER XII.

CHAPTER XIII.

CHAPTER XIV.

CHAPTER XV.

THE

CAPTURE AND ESCAPE.

CHAPTER I.

> Lo, steam, the king with iron steed,
>   Sweeps over many a space,
> Where travellers once, in helpless need,
>   Met Indians face to face.

IN the summer of 1864, long trains of emigrants westward bound, extended along the great highway of the plains from the Missouri River to the rugged mountains of Montana, the fertile valleys of the great basin of Utah, the rich lands of the Columbia, and the grassy slopes of California. The sun poured down his hottest rays upon the vast black hills, oppressing the hardy traveller and weary animals, as they pursued their journey.

They had come from the various States of the great, but then almost divided republic, toiling onward with one aim, seeking new fields of labor and greater room for expansion — pioneers of civilization — the founders

2   13

of Western empire — the hardy sons of toil, whose footsteps disturbed the beaver in his quiet haunts, drove from his abode the grisly bear, and limited the range of the buffalo and prairie-wolf, braving the vengeance of the savage, and turning the dreary wilderness into a garden, causing the desert waste to bloom like the rose.

At the camping-grounds, as they stopped for the evening rest and refreshment, they seemed to represent whole towns of hardy adventurers, filling the scene with life and animation. Gladly they hailed the sun's decline, and temporary relief from clouds of heated dust, as the last rays gilded the tops of the rolling hills that stretched far away until they joined a vast chain of mountains, the lofty summits of which are lost in the purple and golden hues of sunset. Bright harbinger of their future prosperity and glory! and, like the pillar of fire in the wilderness to the children of Israel, it pointed to the promised land.

The pleasant rest of evening, after the day's toil through sun and dust, came gratefully, as the cool winds blew softly over the wide prairies or lofty hills, and little birds warbled their evening songs and fluttered among the waving grass or craggy peaks, and rosy, laughing children, freed from the restraints of confinement in the wagons, ran sporting around. The tired animals, loosed from their harness, lazily cropped the pastures about the encampments, while their owners prepared the evening meal, and enjoyed the twilight hour.

Their road lay over an extensive country of varying soil, and sometimes the travellers were compelled to rest through the night where water and vegetation were scarce, while at others a richly pastured valley and abundance of water invited repose.

Among the many emigrant trains travelling over that great highway was one to which the narrator of these adventures belonged.

As I begin to recount the pleasures and sorrows of our journey across the plains, my pen almost falters; for much that to me is painfully true, and is remembered with bitter recollection, will be to the reader but a tale that is told. I pause, and almost fear to traverse, even in fancy, the backward path that leads through so many sad recollections.

In the year 1859 my husband concluded to remove from Pennsylvania, our native State, to the West, and we bade our many friends adieu, and set out upon our journey. At the separation from the home I loved, one lingering look was cast upon the house and grounds of my earliest and dearest recollections.

Home is the place to which the heart is apt to turn in adversity, and memory see to the latest days of life, though oceans should roll and mountains rise between; and the china horse and doll are remembered in the busy throngs of earth.

Our journey was a safe one, and, after making a visit with our friends in Iowa, we concluded to emigrate to Kansas, and were accompanied thither by my mother and her family. We located in Iola, a town situated in the beautiful valley of the Neosho River. This Territory was then impoverished by drought, and consequently famine, and before these blighting influences had been conquered, the evil effects of war were made manifest.

Conflicting interests divided the population, and bitter feelings separated nearest friends. My husband, in the loyalty of his heart, believed it to be his duty to risk his life in defence of the land he loved and his country's honor. He was chosen lieutenant, and in that capacity served upon the borders of his own State and in Missouri, but the exposures of a camp life proved too severe for him. He was taken with a serious illness, from which he only partially recovered, and, leaving the army, he returned to Iola, where he remained in an ailing and delicate state of health for two years, when his physicians assured him that a change of climate was necessary to the recovery of his health; and although this involved the sacrifice of friends and home comforts, it was cheerfully undertaken with the great object of a restoration in view.

Our first encampment was made in the beautiful valley of the Neosho, May 17th, 1864. As I looked back upon my adopted home far down in the valley, my heart swelled with contending emotions — a thousand reflections crowded upon my memory. I had bid farewell to friends and home to traverse an unknown country — was leaving a fond parent and dear brothers and sisters, to cast my lot with the pioneers of civilization — giving up the tried and true to plunge into unknown and untried associations.

Memory grew busy as I reclined upon a little knoll overlooking the winding stream that threaded like a silver band the fertile valley that I had only a few months before regarded as a place for our home in our temporary sojourn upon earth.

As I contemplated, too, the scene before me, the picture of the home of my childhood, long left to strangers, came like a forgotten dream before my mind, and in fancy I stood once more upon the banks of the Shenango, where, years ago, even before my dear father was laid in the church-yard grave, I gathered wild flowers, and never dreamed that future years would bring anything less bright than the gay blossoms I twined amid my hair.

The next morning we pursued our journey, and the fourth day arrived at the city of Lawrence, just recovering from the dreadful shock of the merciless massacre and destruction inflicted by Quantrell and his murderous band of marauders.

The ruined walls of once elegant buildings frowned dark and gloomy, still showing the marks of the smoke of the consuming fire that destroyed them. As we passed these grim monuments of man's remorseless hatred, I recalled the beautiful lines of Campbell:

> "On Susquehanna's side, fair Wyoming,
>   Although the wild flowers on thy ruined wall
> And roofless homes a sad remembrance bring
>   Of what thy people did befall,
> Yet thou wast once the loveliest land of all."

From Lawrence we travelled across the country to

the Blue River, now noted for Indian outrages perpetrated upon the peaceful and unprotected settlers, and from thence to Fort Kearny, in Nebraska. At this place our road came to the southern bank of the Platte River.

In seasons of high water this river assumes a beautiful appearance; its broad bosom is dotted with islands of richest verdure, and adorned with gorgeous-hued flowers and delicate vining vegetation. These islands are of the height of the adjacent shores, having been formed by the action of the changing currents. that have forced their way around them. Some are miles in length, while others are mere dots of verdure on the breast of the broad water.

Near Fort Kearny the emigrant trains from various parts of the country concentrated, and the scene upon the banks of the river was beautiful — the green literally dotted with white wagon-covers, and the rich pasture numbered thousands of horses and cattle, resting in the lovely valley, before attempting the passage of the plains and penetrating the unknown heights of the rocky peaks that rise beyond.

From this place hundreds of persons with their teams and herds sometimes travelled together, considering that it was prudent to be in large companies while pursuing their journey to the valley of the saints, the mountains of Montana, or the western slope of the long chain whose base is washed by the waters of the Pacific Ocean; while others were seen going in small companies or alone, that the clouds of dust

A VIEW OF THE PLAINS AND THE SOUTH PLATTE RIVER.

that are nowhere more annoying than on the plains, where there were lines of wagons, sometimes extending farther than the eye could range, might be avoided. And it being the time when the fearful struggle was agitating our country, conflicting sentiments of political disturbers were sometimes met with violence and danger, which it was also desirable to avoid. Kearny town was passed three miles west of Fort Kearny. It was a small village, built of adobe or sunburnt brick, and was then in its pristine glory, but now is remembered as a town of the past.

Our road lay along the Platte River for one hundred and eighty miles, without a tree or bush to break the horizon of plain or sky, except a few cottonwoods and willows, which stood like solitary sentinels guarding the magnificent stream that meanders through the valley.

Each day brought its burden of care and toil, while night offered the balmy sweetness of repose. At Cottonwood Springs there was a settlement of some magnitude, and a military post. There all the wagons that belonged to emigrants were searched by officers and soldiers detailed for that purpose, in order to recover any Government arms that might be clandestinely carried away. We continued to pass ranches, at intervals of ten or fifteen miles. These ranchmen were clever, energetic men, who dared to live a frontier life, and often proved themselves to be of the bravest and most generous. Some of them aspired to comfort and even luxury. As a general thing, their houses were built one story high, of adobe or sod, and large enough to accommodate quite a number of guests.

In winter, the ranchmen offer accommodations for travellers and their·teams; but in the season in which we made their acquaintance their hospitality was not so much required, as the travellers usually slept in their wagons, and their animals were turned loose to find pasture.

Many needful things, however, could be purchased of them, as they invariably kept useful articles for sale. One of these ranchmen, a Mr. Morrow, had, disregarding the prevailing custom, built his house two stories high; and having given attention to its completion, produced a residence in the far West that would have done honor to an Eastern farm of pretentious extent.

One hundred and eighty miles from Fort Kearny was the fording of the Platte, where the first California emigrants crossed, and in consequence it is called the "Old California Crossing." At that place we overtook seemingly thousands of persons, with their flocks and teams, encamped in the valley; for that being the warmest season, the snow was melting on the mountains, causing the river to be high.

The Platte, though over a thousand miles in length, is a shallow stream, and would be fordable at almost any place, if it were not for the quicksands, which render it extremely dangerous.

It is subject to great variations, however — now fearfully rapid and broad, inundating the adjacent valley, then sinking into an insignificant stream, running through a desert; and, at other times, except the main channel, disappearing in the porous strata of its bed, leaving only here and there a pond inhabited by small fish and tadpoles.

Some of the islands were covered with wild fruits, plums and grapes growing there in abundance, enjoying the security of isolation from the dry country, which is sometimes swept by fire that destroys every species of vegetation that it meets with remorseless fury.

Sufficient water for family use was obtained by digging pits two or three feet into the ground, which soon filled with cold water — a refreshing beverage that is very desirable when on a toilsome journey.

To cross a wide and rapid stream without the aid of a boat or bridge, was a feat requiring some ingenuity; and after no little consideration, the men took the wheels from the wagons, and placed the boxes upon the water, and filled them with their own wheels and former loading, which was equal to transforming the wagons into boats or rafts. Though peculiar in appearance, these newly made boats soon floated to the other side, transporting very many persons, of all ages, from the infant at its mother's breast to the bowed form and silvered head of the old, to a wilder and less explored country than the plains they had left.

The day *we* crossed, the air was very heavy and oppressively hot. When we were upon the river, the sky began suddenly to darken, and, just as we arrived upon the opposite side, a gleam of lightning, like a forked tongue of flame, shot from the black cloud that w—— rapidly overspreading the heavens. This f——re was followed by a frightful peal of thunder—— ——ated flashes and peals followed them in quick ——, and dense blackness lowered threatenin—— ——, almost shutting out the heights beyond, an—— ——to encircle us like prisoners in the valley that —— at their base.

The vivid flashes that lit this darkness for an instant only caused the gloom to seem more fearful, while the heavy rolling of the thunder seemed to rend the heavens above us. Suddenly the cloud burst upon our unprotected heads in rain. But such rain! not the gentle droppings of an afternoon shower, nor the pattering of a commonplace storm, but a sweeping avalanche of water that drenched everything at the first dash, and, continuing to pour, seemed to threaten the earth, and tempt the mighty river to rise and claim it for its own.

The wagons had been uncovered, that they might be transported with convenience; consequently there were no shelters from the storm, and its fury was exhausted upon us; and while it continued to pour, we were compelled to endure its violence, but awaited in resignation the wrath of the elements, and endeavored to cherish a hope of a bright to-morrow — in which we were not disappointed, for as the sun rose above the hills, smiling upon the world as if nothing unusual had occurred, and kindly kissed the lingering drops from the blades of grass we were winding our way among the hills.

CHAPTER II.

ABOUT twenty miles above the Old California Crossing of the South Platte, the town of Julesburg stood, upon the south bank of the river. This town took its name from a French pioneer, Jules Benard, who built a cabin of sods close by the river, and lived a hermit's life, subsisting upon the fish he could procure from the river, and game that he was able to shoot upon the hills.

It was said his early years had been darkened by misfortune, when he left his home in the East and sought a solace in isolation.

He was described as a kind, honorable old man. When increasing travel on the road to the mountains and Pacific coast enabled him to dispose of his supplies of game and furs, he dealt honorably by emigrants, winning their confidence and esteem, and finally held a position of trust with the overland stage company.

The dreadful mode of his death being the consequence of his refusing to league himself with crime and cruelty, renders it proper that his fate be held in remembrance by posterity.

A desperado, named Slade, who afterward distinguished himself as a bandit in the Rocky Mountains,

23

and was executed by a vigilance committee in Virginia City, Montana, in 1863, made a haunt for crime in the vicinity of Jules' home. His house soon became a scene of robbery and theft, and against such outrages Jules protested, positively refusing to become a party or accomplice in it. For this courageous resistance the old man lost his life.

With a fiendish barbarity that no Indian can outdo, Slade, with a party of his comrades, went to the hermit's house in the night, and, finding him unsuspecting and unarmed, bound him with strong cords, and commenced to mutilate his body — first cutting off his nose, then his fingers, toes, and ears — and continued to disjoint him until death mercifully rescued him from their demon hands.

The town that bore his name has been destined, like its founder, to suffer great changes. In February, 1865, it was burned by Indians, commanded by a noted warrior called Little Dog. An effort was made by our soldiers, who were stationed in a camp near Julesburg, to repulse the enemy and protect the place, but they were unsuccessful, and twenty-five soldiers were killed. Fort Sedgwick was soon afterward erected near its ruins, and the subsequent year a town was built four miles to the east, near the Nebraska line, and named Julesburg. The growth of *this* town, however, was not flourishing, for the Great Pacific Railroad caused another town to be suggested, which was also called Julesburg. This town was destined to become quite a prodigy in growth and wickedness.

Within the short space of six weeks it sprang into

existence, and covered an area of three hundred acres. Of twelve hundred houses, nine hundred were saloons. Over the streets, that had scarcely ceased to be paths in the wilderness, Government trains passed, bound for distant frontier forts. Railway employes, with long lines of wagons containing implements and necessaries for the great work going on farther west; ox-trains, en route for the gold regions, transporting merchandise; drivers flourishing long whips, and shouting with all the force of their powerful lungs — kept up a varying procession; and the vile exhilarant called whisky was freely used, and aided much in causing the wild excitement.

Denver, when in its greatest excitement, did not equal the progress of this place. A person unaccustomed to Western phenomena cannot realize the confusion that prevailed.

The majority of the nine hundred saloons were devoted to gambling, and most of the known games on the earth were played there. Every device by which money could be lost or squandered was rife, and recklessness and prodigality reigned.

There was no law, not even a respectable vigilance committee; and being out of the pale of recognized authority, except the military, which seemed to fear and tremble, terrible encounters with bowie-knives and other formidable weapons were frequent, and all the men carried firearms to defend themselves in case of an attack. Fancied insults were often atoned for with blood, and tragedies were daily events. Fortunes

3

were lost at a single sitting at the gambling table; temptation led men away, in the flush of sudden success, to renewed recklessness, while despair seized others and hurried them to crime.

In the midst of these frightful excesses a corrupt power was born, and added despotism to confusion. A band of desperate-minded men proclaimed themselves law-abiding citizens, and proceeded to form a code of laws for the benefit of the city government, and organized a bogus court to dispense justice, or, properly, injustice.

A grievous tax was levied, and, in many instances, collected by coercion, and a license was required on all business and labor, no exceptions being made in favor of even the few poor laboring women, some of whom, alas! were, by this unreasonable taxation, driven to desperation.

Drugged liquors were given to teamsters and others whose wages were sufficiently tempting to excite the cupidity of some of these desperadoes; they were then arrested for drunkenness or some other crime, and hurried to prison, and there robbed of their hard-earned money, and, in some cases, beaten and threatened with violence if they revealed the facts, or even entered the town after being released from prison.

But, notwithstanding, men generally followed the inclinations of their own hearts, and the boldest took, as it were, their lives in their hands, and bravely dared consequences.

A theatre was established, where a motley audience,

dressed in every conceivable fashion, and of every grade of character but the pure, came together nightly to witness melodramas no less startling than their own lives.

If ever the preaching of the gospel might claim a field rife in iniquity, since the days when the great Baptist cried from the wilderness of Judea, "Repent ye, for the kingdom of heaven is at hand," surely this was one. Missionaries are sent over the stormy seas to learn the languages of dusky nations that sit in darkness, that they may be able to proclaim to them the glad tidings of salvation; but those of our own nation, speaking our own language, and having the smothered seed of Christian knowledge in their hearts through the dim recollection of early teachings, rush to ruin, without heeding the loving warning, "Repent ye, why will ye die?" Yet be it said for the Western prairies, as a general thing, their towns are not churchless.

The questionable advancement of Julesburg was of short duration. Like its predecessors, it has sunk into insignificance. As the Union Pacific Railroad progressed, other towns sprang into existence farther West, and divided its prosperity, until the inhabitants, seeing the futility of remaining at Julesburg, followed the work, and the city of prodigy, that passed from infancy to old age in the short space of a few weeks, having polled in the mean time four thousand votes, vanished like a morning dew, and the ground was almost deserted in three months from the time of its commencement.

This ephemeral city, whose glory was so short, was located on a sandy plain, with a few hillocks rising around, and some craggy heights visible in the neighborhood toward the north, and the Platte River, two miles distant, to the southward.

A story is told of two Indian chiefs, Spotted Tail and Big Mouth, meeting, at Julesburg, a member of the English Parliament, who, like themselves, had come to see the city that had flashed into existence in the Western wilderness, where a few days before the prairie-wolf lay safely in its haunts, and the buffalo grazed upon its favorite pastures.

The English lord and his party determined to visit the red man's lodge, and, taking an interpreter, they departed under the escort of the chiefs, who, believing their guests were persons of distinction, tendered them every honor, and the best entertainment their camp afforded. Big Mouth, being especially interested with the courteous visitors, begged that the English lord would accept a memento of his kind feelings which could be carried beyond the great waters. To this the nobleman assented, when, behold! the proud chieftain led forward a young squaw, his daughter, and offered her in marriage; but, being the husband of a fair lady, with many thanks and some embarrassment the gentlemanly stranger declined the precious gift.

Cheyenne City stands one hundred and seventeen miles west of Julesburg. In its commencement it flourished after the style of its predecessor, but, after some reverses, settled down into a moderately thrifty town.

But I have diverged quite far enough from my narrative, as it was not the history of the far West that was intended for this volume.

CHAPTER III.

TWENTY-FIVE miles from California Crossing,
we came to Ash Hollow, where General Harney,
some years before, had immortalized his name by an
indiscriminate slaughter of Indians — men, women,
and children — supposed to be hostile.

Court-house Rock is probably the next object of
interest that attracts the attention of the traveller. It
stands out in bold relief, several miles from the road
that leads from the Crossing to Fort Laramie, and not
far from a stream of water called Pumpkin Creek,
which is supplied from the numerous springs and
snows of the mountains, and is always flowing with
abundance of pure water. In its valley timber is
found in sufficient quantities to meet the demand.
Eight miles to the southward of our camp, in glorious
grandeur, was seen this result of a wonderful freak of
nature, and object of much curiosity. It rises grandly
from its base at the level of the water in the neighboring creek, six hundred feet to its summit, in
the form of a pyramid, reminding one of the work

3 *   29

of Titans, or antedeluvian giants, that might have erected it for a lookout from which to watch and guard the surrounding country, or for a monument to survive their day and record their existence.

The view from its summit is extremely grand. To the northwest can be seen the strange and singular outlines of Chimney Rock, and the rolling hills beyond. To the southward, immediately at its base, is a chasm or abyss, in the depths of which the view is lost in darkness.

Court-house Rock is a compound or composite of clay and sandstone, and is so soft as to be easily detached by cutting instruments, and many persons have availed themselves of this advantage by making upon its steep sides steps by which to ascend to the summit. It is a perilous undertaking, though many have succeeded in accomplishing the feat, as their names bear testimony, for the steep sides were covered with names in all styles of chirography.

When this rock is seen from a few miles' distance, it appears to those unacquainted with rarefied atmosphere, peculiar to the plains, to be near and of insignificant dimensions; thus deluding the travellers who sometimes undertake to walk over to examine it; but the mistake is eventually discovered, and the enthusiastic investigator returns to his camp in disgust with the deceptive appearance of the country, and postpones his visit until a more suitable conveyance than he had engaged can be procured.

Court-house Rock derived its name from its fancied resemblance to some magnificent ruin. From some views it strongly reminds one of the pictures of old cathedrals, or frowning battlements of the structures built in the dark ages, which have lost a portion of their symmetry by the ruthless hand of time.

Eighteen miles west of Court-house Rock is Chimney Rock, an equally curious phenomenon, and is formed of the same material — sand and clay. It is in the form of a shaft or pillar, and springs from the apex of a cone, and is three hundred and eighty feet in height. Chimney Rock stands five hundred feet from a bluff, of which it seems to have once formed a portion. At its base is a stratum of limestone. This rock is gradually crumbling away.

Fifteen miles farther west is Fortification Rock, near Scott's Bluffs. A spur from Scott's Bluffs extends to the river, compelling the traveller to leave the stream and make a detour southward.

The passage through the bluffs is very intricate and dangerous for teams to pass, and at times the drifting sands almost obscure the high walls which rise several hundred feet on either side. Cedar and pine trees are seen growing from the crevices, or standing apparently upon the naked rocks, even to the summit of these rugged walls. To a person below, these trees seem to be insignificant shrubs, but upon near inspection they are found to be trees of large dimensions.

Near these bluffs, Captain Shoeman has since erected Fort Mitchell, one of the most commodious forts in the West.

Twenty miles farther west, we came to Cold Creek, a beautiful stream, about thirty feet wide, which empties into the North Platte. The waters of this creek keep their own side of the channel for several miles before they mingle with the muddy current of the Platte.

Cold Creek abounds with fine trout, which, being unaccustomed to the white man's mode of fishing, are easily decoyed into seines, and thousands of the unsuspicious creatures may be caught in an hour. At our camp on this creek we received a visit from an Indian chief called Good Horse.

This Indian was tall, well-proportioned, and graceful in appearance, and by frequently visiting military stations he had acquired some knowledge of the English language and of civilized manners. His dress consisted of a buffalo-robe, worn loosely around his body, a soldier's hat upon his head, and moccasins upon his feet.

The hat he wore through respect for the white strangers. In his hand he carried a sword; but perceiving that the children feared this weapon, he placed it upon the ground, and at the same time stated that he was a friend to the white man.

Supper was offered him, but, fearing poison, he refused to partake until he had seen the food tasted; then, with many thanks, he ate what was given him, and, feeling reassured, stripped his horse of its saddle and bridle, and turned its head toward his lodges, about a mile distant, when the sagacious animal at once set out for home, where its arrival was understood to be a signal from the chief for his family to join him.

His three wives soon came to the camp, when Good Horse, to display his knowledge of etiquette and civilized customs, introduced them to each one of the company; after which ceremony he intimated that they would eat a little; for "Indian women," said he, "are always hungry." Supper was immediately set for them, of which they heartily partook, and, rising from the ground, they promptly informed us that they would eat at the other fires too.

It seems to be a prominent trait in Indian character never to refuse an invitation to eat; and their promptness to accept invitations to partake of a meal has impressed many travellers with the belief that it is their peculiar mode of showing friendship.

Darkness had set in upon us. The pony was brought back. The chief shook hands with each one of us, mounted his horse — which had been saddled in the mean time by one of his wives — and rode away, leaving his wives to follow on foot. Such is Indian gallantry.

But this was not the last we saw of them. Early the next morning they returned, but were not as courteous as they had been on the evening previous.

Some presents offered them were accepted in silence. The chief, discovering that the travellers were not inclined to be as liberal as he anticipated, told us he had not come to talk, but to beg — the visiting hav-

C

ing been done the evening before; and requested that we would be as prompt and liberal as possible, and refrain from annoying his wives by talking to them.

They asked for breakfast, and, after eating, solicited some food to carry to their children. They seemed particularly fond of milk, and when the supply was exhausted, insisted that more be procured.

We had read much of the noble character of the red man, of his lofty bearing, scorn, pride, etc., all of which our acquaintance with Good Horse and his family failed to confirm.

Seventeen miles from Cold Creek was a ranch, and five miles farther west Fort Laramie is located. This fort is one of the oldest in the country. It is said the location was selected by some trappers for their head-quarters and a trading-post, where they kept up a traffic, many years ago, with the Indians. Although it was in an exposed position, it was not surrounded by an enclosure. There was great simplicity, too, in its arrangements, and its regulations were so well adapted to circumstances that the Indians did not feel themselves held at a distance from the Government agents, whose prejudices did not forbid them from taking the swarthy children of the wilderness into their sympathy; and, although they were the enemy they had left their homes to fight, they were friendly to them, and many of the officers, as well as common soldiers, had taken of the swarthy daughters for wives. Though the Indian women universally refuse to speak

the English language, and are wild and peculiar in
their habits, they were sometimes good housekeepers,
and kind and affectionate to those around them; and
the soldiers, absent from their dear ones at home,
doubtless found a solace in their company; and as the
Indian language is not difficult to understand, they
soon conversed intelligibly. To a stranger the fort
presented a lively, if not interesting appearance.
Walking, standing, or sitting in the shadows of the
houses, singly or in groups, could be seen these Indian
women and their children, chatting and playing with
each other — pitiable-looking children of aboriginal
descent, half surrounded by civilization, yet held in
the lap of barbarity, smiling upon fair fathers, yet
kissed by swarthy mothers. Some of these children
were of fair complexion, with pleasant countenances,
and, under dissimilar circumstances, might have been
deemed of Saxon descent. They were dressed in every
conceivable style, or not dressed at all, just as the
mother's fancy dictated. The skill of the mother was
mostly displayed in the decorative art, and various
colored paints, glass beads, tin and brass wire, and
scarlet strings, etc., were displayed in confusion. Possibly many a fond father's heart has beaten with pride
at the sight of his little son decorated with feathers,
etc., and grotesquely spotted with vermilion, in the
style of an Indian juggler; and, doubtless, he must
have felt a peculiar sensation of satisfaction at behold-
ing the beauty of the countenance, if a sting of re-
morse would not interfere with the thought of the

destiny that awaited his child, when the Government should demand the presence of its natural protector in another field of action, when the Indian mother would return to her own people, to train the child for war and revenge against his father's race. Or if it be a daughter, who can contemplate the life she must lead? The Indian women about the fort follow in their style of costumes a sort of compromise between the customs of Indians and the fashions of civilization, in which gaudy-colored calico, beads, brass wire, shawls, buffalo robes, and blankets mingle in intricate confusion, making it very difficult for an observer to determine whether the woman has on a dress or a calico shirt, whether she wears a skirt or leggins; and although the head is always uncovered, their heavy black tresses are usually without ornament. The hair is parted in the middle of the head, confined with two braids, and allowed to hang down behind the ears. The parting of the hair is always painted with some bright-colored paint, which is also bountifully distributed over the face; and many of them display a star tattooed upon the forehead; and the quantity and variety of glass beads worn around the neck is truly a marvel — their whole appearance strongly resembling a display of figures in a museum, or persuading one that a second-handed store had been appropriated for their use.

This fort, like many others in the West, was not well supplied with water — the Laramie River, on which it is built, being the only resource. The parade-

ground presented a barren appearance, being unre-
lieved by any vegetation, with the exception of two
small pine-trees that stood to the southward, endeavoring to retain their former beauty and usefulness.
They were objects of much interest, being the only
trees in the immediate neighborhood, except a little
grove upon the banks of the Laramie River to the
southward of the fort, which would have been a delightful place of resort had it not been for the disagreeable use to which it had been appropriated — a
burying-place for Indian dead. It had been used for
that purpose a long time, judging from the remains
scattered upon the ground under the trees, from which
they had fallen in the process of decay, when leaving
their place among the boughs to some future occupant
to lay in and moulder away under the action of time
and the elements, and to be displaced in turn by
decay, leaving the place again unoccupied.

The fort is situated on the river, about two miles
from where it empties into the North Platte, and at
the base of a succession of hills, above whose heights
is seen Laramie Peak, which rises grandly sixteen
thousand feet above the level of the sea.

Forty miles from Fort Laramie is Horse-shoe Creek,
where had lived the noted desperado Slade, with his
wife, a lady of respectability. At this place a fort was
afterward erected by Captain Marshall, and subsequently burned by Indians.

Twenty-five miles farther west is another stream,

4

that offered a pleasant place for the weary strangers' encampment. Twelve miles still farther was a creek called Laparrall; this stream was overshadowed by a luxuriant growth of timber, and the lovely valley was covered with grass and dotted with wild fruits and flowers. Eight miles from that place is the memorable Little Box-Elder Creek.

CHAPTER IV.

CROSSING OF LITTLE BOX-ELDER — SUDDEN APPEARANCE
OF INDIANS — PREPARATIONS FOR DEFENCE — TOKIT-
CHEY'S ASSURANCES OF FRIENDSHIP — THEIR SINGULAR
CONDUCT — ATTACK AND PLUNDER OF THE WAGONS.

THE evening of the 12th of July we had already
been many weeks on our toilsome journey. The
weather was excessively warm, and with the decline
of the sun we looked forward to the cool of approaching night, with a sense of relief from the oppressive
heat of the day. Slowly our wagons wound through
the timber that skirted the Little Box-Elder Creek,
and, crossing the stream, ascended the opposite bank.
We had no thought of danger, nor timid misgivings
on the subject of the Indians: any we might have felt
at starting from home were all scattered by the constantly received assurances of their friendship. At
the outposts and ranches we passed we had heard
nothing but ridicule of their pretensions to warfare,
and at Fort Laramie, where reliable information was
expected, renewed pledges of the safety of the road were
given. At Horse-shoe Creek, which had been passed
three days previous, was a telegraph office, and, in answer to our inquiries, we received similar declarations
as to the quiet and peaceful state of the country through

which we must pass.   Being thus persuaded that fears
were useless, we entertained none, and preferred to
travel in small companies, to avoid confusion and
dust, that always attend the presence and movements
of a large emigrant train.

Our train consisted of eleven persons, five wagons,
and a herd of loose stock.   The persons were one Mr.
Kelley and his wife and child, a Mr. Wakefield, a Mr.
Sharp, and three hired men, besides Mr. Larimer, our
child, and myself.

The beauty of the sunset and the scenery around
filled us with admiration as we viewed the grand peaks
before us, tinged in purple and gold, without a thought
of the danger that was lying like a tiger in ambush by
our path.

It will be borne in mind by my readers that the
Indian war, which has since been carried on with more
than usual success by the Sioux and their auxiliaries,
had not then commenced, our train being the first one
attacked, and with it commenced the war that has not
yet been brought to a close. Suddenly, without a sound
to warn us of danger, the bluffs before us were covered
with a party of about two hundred and fifty Indians,
painted and equipped for the war-path, who uttered a
wild cry and fired a volley from their guns into the air.

This terrible and unsuspected apparition came upon
us with such startling swiftness that we had no time
to make preparations for defence before the main body
halted and sent out a small force, which encircled us
and stationed themselves at regular intervals, but at a

distance of about one hundred and fifty yards from the wagons, thus completely surrounding our train — the larger body remaining in its position upon the elevation in front, apparently determining upon some mode of action.

Our men immediately halted the teams and formed a corral of the wagons, and gathered their arms for defence, my husband particularly advising a determined resistance. His knowledge of Indian character had taught him that prompt action is the only safeguard against Indian treachery. But feeling conscious of our helpless situation, I remonstrated against a single shot being fired, fearing to provoke an attack, which, though probable, was not a certainty, and entreated them to forbear, as I believed a successful defence was impossible in such an unequal contest, and death would be certain if they attempted resistance; and begging a conciliatory course as the only hope, I held my child in my arms, and awaited in breathless anxiety the result.

The ready facility with which the wagons were corralled, and the hasty preparations for defence, most likely intimidated the savages somewhat, who are brave when life is comparatively safe; but it is not consistent with their mode of warfare to expose themselves too much, for they are chary of life, always watchful, and striking when least expected.

Our son, little Frank, from the commencement of our journey, had entertained an ungovernable dread of the Indians — a repugnance that could not be over-

4*

come, although in our intercourse with friendly Indians I had endeavored to show him how unfounded his fears were, and persuade him that they were civil and harmless — but in vain.

Never can I forget the expression upon his countenance, when the savages came upon us, as he looked up into my face, saying, "Mother, I want to pray." It had been his custom to kneel at my side, in the evening, with little hands folded, and raise his innocent petitions to our Heavenly Father, whose protecting love seemed nearer to him in the wilderness than in his own little chamber at home; and now he turned to the same strong arm, and his pure faith came like a drop of balm into the bitter fear and lowering trouble surrounding us. When the last words of his little prayer were ended, he looked up and said, "Now, mother, shall I go to sleep?" Laying him down in the wagon, I covered his nestling form under the bedclothing, trusting to conceal him from the Indians' sight. Soon after, I saw my husband go out to meet the chief and demand his intentions.

The savage leader immediately advanced, uttering the word, "How! how!" and, placing his hand upon his breast, he said in English: "Good Indian;" and, pointing toward his men, he added: "Heap good Indian — hunt buffalo, antelope, and deer;" then offered his hand, with the usual salutation of his people, "How! how!" and, turning in his saddle, he motioned for his men to advance and follow his example, which they did, and were soon crowding around the wagons, nodding and smiling, with very many demonstrations of good will.

This deception did not relieve our suspicions; yet our only policy seemed to be in temporizing, in hope that assistance might approach; but this was a feeble hope, as they grew ominously familiar, examining the mouths of the horses, and the manner by which the harness was attached to them, etc. Though it was extremely warm weather, some of them affected to tremble with cold, offering that as a reason why they wished to take goods from the wagons. Many of them were only partially dressed, the body being entirely naked to the waist, except a coat of paint. Their heads were invariably uncovered, and their feet dressed with moccasins.

Many presents were offered and accepted; but some were only taken to cast away. Their communications were quite intelligible, being always accompanied by signs, and in several instances by the English language, which some of them seemed to be quite familiar with. Being anxious to preserve a friendly intercourse as long as possible, they were permitted to detain us without remonstrance on our part. Finally the chief—whom I will call Tokitchey—intimated that he desired that the wagons would go farther; and fearing to gain his displeasure by seeming disobedience or disregard of his wish, and being anxious to escape from the fearful spot, the men concluded to move on, and the train was soon in motion, the Indians insisting upon assisting to drive the herd.

When we had gone but a few rods, it was discovered that we were approaching a deep, rocky glen, in whose gloomy depths a murderous attack was probable, and from which escape would be impossible; and a halt was called. Although the savages insisted we should proceed, we persisted, and again formed a corral of the wagons.

Tokitchey, seeing the futility of further persistence, with equal cunning solicited supper for himself and his men, declaring that when they had partaken they would immediately depart for the hills, leaving us alone in our encampment.

Though to prepare a meal for two hundred and fifty Indians was not a small undertaking, the work was soon in progress. When all the men were busily engaged, the savages, deeming it a favorable opportunity, threw off their mask of friendship, and displayed their true character and intentions. At this moment, Mr. Larimer was engaged in making a fire, and Mr. Kelley and two colored men were preparing the meal. These negroes had been slaves among the Cherokees, and understood the Indian character by personal observation, and their fear, at this time, was unbounded, and pitiable even to us who shared the danger.

Mr. Wakefield and Mr. Taylor were busy with the teams. Mr. Sharp, who was aged and almost blind, and was trembling with fear, had, from the first, made every effort to gain the good will of the Indians, and was now distributing his store of sugar among them, and urging our men to move on in accordance with their request. An Indian approached, and took a gun from near my side. To this I objected in vain. At this instant there was a simultaneous discharge of arms, which were followed by the fearful war-whoop and hideous shouts. For one moment there was seeming confusion, but in another I perceived that they worked with perfect order, and as the cloud of smoke cleared away, each Indian could be seen busily engaged, but not one of our men was in sight. My impression was they had all escaped unhurt, and I immediately determined upon a course of action. Well knowing that entreaties would be of no avail with the savages, and any indiscreetness on my part might result in jeopardizing our lives, I endeavored to suppress my fears, and with an air of indifference commenced to assist them to unload the wagon I was in. With miraculous rapidity the Indians had mounted into the wagons and commenced the work of distributing and destroying the contents, using their tomahawks to pry open trunks and boxes, which they split up in savage recklessness. Mrs. Kelley kept her seat in the wagon until her presence was regarded as irksome, when the chief threw her violently to the ground and dragged her some distance, while the terrified child was left to climb from the wagon and follow her. I was soon told that my services were not required, and I was at liberty to join my companions. When walking with my child toward my frightened friends, doubtless some signs of alarm were manifest in our appearance, for the chief placed his hand upon his

revolver and cast a savage, if not murderous look upon
us. Fearing his vengeance, we proceeded to advance,
but instantly I resolved upon a plan to escape, and
would have put it in execution but for the helplessness
of the child, who, I feared, would fail in the attempt.
Yet, notwithstanding, we made a few steps sidewise
for the purpose of starting hastily toward the timber;
but the vigilant eye of the savage chieftain was immediately upon us, and in an authoritative manner he called,
in English, saying, "Come back!" Realizing the
futility of a present effort, I obeyed, and, approaching
the savage, asked him for protection, which he did not
seem inclined to promise that we should have; but,
although he gave us no assurance of kindness that we
could comprehend, he presented Mrs. Kelley with a
wreath of gay-colored feathers, which we supposed he
wore for ornament, when in reality it was a token of
favor and assurance to her of his protecting care. He
then left us, in order to secure his portion of the
plunder — not, however, until a special guard had been
placed near us. Night came upon us, and darkness
closed over the scene of destruction before their
arrangements for departure were completed. The
first intimation we had that our immediate massacre
was not intended was a few articles of clothing presented by a boy, who intimated that we would have
need for them. Among the confused mass of material
of all kinds scattered about was a package of letters
that the young Indian also brought and gave us,
which suggested to me a plan, and I eagerly accepted

them, to strew upon the way if we should be taken with the Indians, hoping they would be a guide for our pursuing friends, or for us, if we should escape and endeavor to retrace our steps. Many things which the Indians could not carry with them they gathered into a pile and lighted. The light of the flames showed us the forms of our captors busily loading the horses with plunder and preparing to depart. When their arrangements were completed, they came to us and signified that they were ready to go, and that we must accompany them. This was the first reliable assurance they gave us that our lives were not in immediate danger, and we hailed it gratefully, for with the prospect of life hope revived, and faith to believe that God had not forsaken us, and that we might yet be united to our friends, who never seemed dearer than when we were about to be carried into captivity.

Many persons have since assured me that death would have been preferable to life with such prospects, saying that rather than have submitted to be carried away by savages to a doubtful doom, they would have taken their own lives; but it is only those who have looked over the dark abyss of death that know how the soul shrinks from meeting the unknown future. For while hope offers the faintest token of regard, we pause upon the fearful brink of eternity and look back for rescue.

My son, little Frank, caught my hand and murmured, "Oh, mother, I don't want to go, I don't want to go," and his trembling form and half-stifled sobs betrayed his grief. I suppressed my own emotions, and with a low whisper of caution silenced his sobs, for I feared the Indians would not brook any expressions of grief without inflicting summary punishment, and only awaited a pretext to sacrifice us to their rapacious thirst for blood.

I climbed into the saddle, and looking back, saw my little, helpless child in the midst of the blood-thirsty savages, and feared to claim him lest I should provoke their anger or give them a pretext to take his life; but the pleading face of my trembling child overcame my dread, and, extending my arms, I begged imploringly for him: one moment they hesitated, and then placed him upon the horse with me.

The air was cool, and the sky was bright with the glitter of stars. The water of the creek, as it fell over the rocks in the distance, came to our ears with a faint murmur. All nature seemed pitiless in its calm repose, unconscious of our desolation.

The cry of the night-birds and hum of insects came with painful clearness as we turned to leave the valley of Little Box-Elder. With anxious eyes we strove to penetrate the shadows of the woods where we thought our friends might have taken refuge.

The smouldering ruins of much of our property had fallen into ashes, the smoke had faded away, and night had covered the traces of confusion and death.

CHAPTER V.

AS I proceed with my narrative, I must pause and gather up the threads, lest they become a tangled skein, and give events in their order of occurrence, although some of them were not known to me for some time afterward.

When the Indians commenced their murderous attack, Mr. Kelley was startled by the report, and hurriedly glanced around, and saw the pale face of his wife and child in his wagon, and Mr. Sharp fall from the side of his wagon, into which he was reaching. The utter futility of opposing his insignificant strength against two hundred and fifty Indians was apparent. He had laid down his gun to assist in preparing supper, and consequently was unarmed: all he could do was to make a desperate effort to save himself, and he turned and fled for his life.

As he went, the air seemed filled with whizzing arrows. Black Franklin, who was at his side, seemed to stumble, and was left behind. He saw Mr. Larimer and Mr. Wakefield also fall. Soon arriving at some tall grass and small bushes, he concealed himself among

5   D   49

them, and lay crouching and scarcely daring to breathe. He could hear the noise of the chopping and breaking of boxes, and the voices of the Indians calling to each other, and finally the chanting of their monotonous war-song as they took their way across the hills, carrying his yearning thought with them, for he dreaded to dwell upon what might be the fate of his wife and child. At one time he almost resolved to rush back and sacrifice his own life, with no hope of saving them. But his knowledge of Indian character persuaded him that they might be redeemed with money, and he determined to save his own life, with the faint hope of some day rescuing them.

Lying in his perilous shelter, he had seen darkness creep slowly around the hills and close on the scene of destruction and robbery — like a merciful curtain dropped to shut out a hideous sight. Still fearing to move, he heard the sound of cautious footsteps near him, and knew, by the stealthy tread, they were of an Indian.

More closely he crouched to the ground, fearing each instant the descent of the tomahawk and the stroke of the scalping-knife; when, strange to say, a venomous reptile, a rattlesnake, curved its neck close by him, and thrusting forth its poisonous fangs, uttered a warning hiss, and the Indian took alarm and retreated, leaving the fugitive to share the reptile's den unharmed by the bloody knife.

Cautiously he crawled from the weeds and grass, and gaining his feet, started swiftly in an eastern di-

rection, and after travelling eight miles, came to a large
emigrant train that had camped without knowing of the
Indian troubles ahead, but had learned of it through the
report of a family that had arrived on the opposite
side of the creek overlooking the timber, and at about
a mile's distance, when the Indians surrounded us, and
had immediately turned back; and while the driver
encouraged the horses with all his might, his wife
threw out everything she could, to lighten the load:
they succeeded in making their escape uninjured,
though an arrow passed through the sleeve of their infant child's dress. But a horseman that was riding a
few yards in advance was killed.

The news of the massacre spread rapidly, and many
small trains consolidated with the larger one, in order
that a successful resistance might be effected, in case
of an attack.

The colored man, Andy, soon arrived; and not
knowing of the escape of his companion, reported
all his company killed, "and he only left to tell."
Great consternation spread with the tidings of the
massacre; but fears for personal safety prevented any
attempt to chastise the offenders.

This train did not move forward until late the next
morning, and then every necessary precaution was
taken to avoid surprise and secure safety.

Women, in many instances, drove the teams, to
prevent their men being taken at a disadvantage.
Weapons were in order, and vigilant eyes were fixed
upon every bluff and gorge, anticipating an attack.

At noon they stopped for refreshment, and found the body of the horseman, which, when viewed at a little distance, resembled a clump of brushwood, from the feathered arrow-tops sticking from it — ninety arrows having entered it.

The body was placed in a wagon, and the train moved on, and soon arrived at the place of our misfortunes; and, looking around, they saw the traces of senseless havoc and savage brutality. The remains of much that was but half destroyed lay scattered upon the ground, among which were found the dead bodies of three of our company, Mr. Taylor, Mr. Sharp, and Franklin, one of the colored men.

Mr. Taylor had been shot in the forehead, and lay where he fell. The negro had been shot by an arrow that pierced his legs, pinning them together, in which condition he had been murdered by having his skull broken. Mr. Sharp and Mr. Taylor each left a family at home to mourn their loss.

Mr. Larimer was found living, but wounded, an arrow having passed through his thigh near the body. He was faint with the pain of his wound and loss of blood. After falling, he had arisen and proceeded a little farther, where he was overtaken by Mr. Wakefield, who said, "I am mortally wounded; you will find my body among these bushes."

Mr. Larimer proceeded to a secluded place, which he thought might be a tolerably safe retreat, and concealed himself, where he was able to hear the noise of the work of destruction — as the Indians industriously destroyed what they could not take away — and the song, as they left the field of robbery and carnage.

In the night he was startled by the cracking of a twig, that seemed to have yielded to the weight of a footstep; and hearing breathing close by, observed more closely, and discovered an Indian crawling into his seclusion: he drew his revolver and discharged it into his breast, when the savage fell upon the ground. The report having sounded upon the still night air, guided others to the place, and the remainder of that night he spent in endeavoring to elude his savage pursuers. When morning dawned, he was urged, by his anxiety for the fate of his family, to return to the wagons to examine the ruins, although he dreaded to dwell upon what the fearful spot might disclose.

He had proceeded but a short distance, when he discovered Indians lurking among the hills; but, notwithstanding his dangerous position, he hastened to the place, and ascertained the number of the dead and the absence of his family: he then sought the cover of a projecting rock, to await the arrival of travellers that were in the rear the previous day.

After searching the neighborhood for a quarter of a mile from where last seen, Mr. Wakefield was discovered alive, but pierced by three arrows, that he had vainly endeavored to extricate, succeeding only in withdrawing the shafts, leaving the steel points imbedded in the flesh.

He was cared for with all the kindness possible for

5 *

his rescuers to show, and was taken to Fort Deer-Creek, fifteen miles beyond, where he survived eight months.

A grave being dug for the interment of the dead, the four bodies were solemnly consigned, uncoffined, to the earth. A buffalo-robe, that had been left in a wagon, was placed over them, and then the earth was piled upon their unconscious breasts.

At that time the question of color had occasioned very much dissension, and a great deal was being said of the propriety of allowing the black race the privilege of mingling with the white.

But colored Franklin had suffered death with our companions, and was not deemed unworthy to share their grave; and they lay together, where kind strangers left them — the latter meditating, as they pursued their journey, upon the uncertainty of life, and of the high hopes and fearless energy which, doubtless, each one had cherished, after bidding farewell to friends at home, feeling secure in the success that awaited him in the land of gold, and never for a moment dreaming of a grave in the wilderness that was to close over him.

A little mound raised above the level, on which the prairie-wolf can elevate himself above the sea of grass and howl his lonely cry of hunger and disappointment, is all that marks their resting-place, and the passing stranger only says, "There is a grave."

The cattle that had been driven in the herd were found grazing in the valley, and the ox-teams were still tied to the stakes where they had been secured the evening before; and, in their helpless condition, presented a pitiable sight. The sun shone hot, and they had neither food nor drink from the day before, but stood as prisoners among the ruins and the dead.

Very many arrows were found strewn upon the ground, their owners having belonged to the Sioux family, though of various bands. The arrows were of similar form and finish. The shape was round, of about two feet in length, and grooved on three sides, that the blood of its victim might not be impeded in its outward flow. Each was tipped with three feathers, about six inches long. These feathers are used to guide the arrow on its mission of death. The depth of the wound depends somewhat upon the distance of the aim, but the arrow sometimes passes quite through the body, though usually the force is exhausted when it has penetrated a few inches beyond the point.

The wounded being made as comfortable as circumstances would allow, in the wagon of a stranger, the train, now consisting of hundreds of wagons and several hundred persons, moved slowly forward to an encampment at a short distance from the sad place where their fellow-travellers' career had ended forever — whose vision of the golden land must now be higher and brighter than earthly eyes can see.

The next day the large train arrived at the fort, and the wounded men were intrusted to the care of the commandant, Captain Rynheart — as the kind travellers were compelled by military regulations to take their animals beyond the Government reservation, lest the grazing intended for Government stock should be consumed by emigrant herds.

The wounded men were taken from the wagon in which they had been brought, and laid upon the burning sand, without couch or coverlet: even the buffalo-robe that had been buried with the dead would have been a Samaritan gift to the living in that hour of poverty and distress, to have formed a cover for their aching wounds, and protect them from the scorching rays of the sun.

Though the flag of our country floated proudly above the walls, and seemed to beckon for the afflicted, unfortunate, and distressed to come to its shadow and find repose under its folds, they were unwelcome guests, seeming to have no legal claims upon the garrison, and only permitted to enter by act of charity. Finally, a small tent was procured of a mountaineer, which was graciously accepted for a shield from the pitiless rays of the sun; and, by the kindness of soldiers and travellers, much of their suffering was alleviated.

The night of their arrival in the fort, many emigrant women being encamped in the neighborhood, who could be induced to dance, a ball was given; and the lady who so narrowly escaped death or abduction, by riding with her family for their lives, having lost her wardrobe with her trunks, borrowed a dress of Mrs. Holbrook, the wife of a non-commissioned officer, and the only lady residing in the fort, and joined in the festivities, regardless of the sorrow and the gloom that had recently surrounded them — the burial of their companion and our poor men having only been completed. Such seems to be the influence of familiarity with danger, and isolation from social restraint. The heart loses in a measure the gentler sympathies, and a recklessness in everyday habits is sometimes contracted, that is truly appalling to those unaccustomed to such terrific scenes and associations.

CHAPTER VI.

THE Indians left the scene of their cruel rapacity,
travelling to the northward, and chanting their
monotonous war-song. After a ride of two miles,
through tall weeds and small bushes, we left the bottom lands and ascended some bluffs, and soon after
came to a creek which was easily forded, and where
they drank and kindly offered water to us. The hills
beyond began to be more difficult to ascend, and the
gorges seemed fearfully deep, as we looked into the
black shadows that were not relieved by the feeble
light of the stars.

Here Mrs. Kelley conceived a plan for her child's
escape, of which I was unconscious, and whispered,
"Mary, I believe you had better go back; if you
will make the attempt, I will help you to the ground."
The child, trusting in its mother's judgment, readily
consented, and she took the little trembling hand in
her own and lowered her gently from the horse, and
the child lay crouching until, darkness and distance
intervening, she was lost from sight forever. Left

58

alone in the wilderness, a little helpless child, who can portray her terror ?

With faith to trust and courage to dare, that little, trembling form through the long hours of the night kept watch. The lonely cry of the night-bird had no fear in its melancholy scream for the little wanderer who crouched amid the prairie-grass. The baying of the gray wolf, as he passed the lonely watcher, might startle, but could not drive the faith from her heart. Surely God is just, and angels will guide the little, faltering feet to friends and home. Innocent of wrong, how could she but trust that the unseen hands of spirits would guide her from the surrounding peril. It must have been something stronger than a vague hope of liberty, to be lost or won, that guided the feeble steps of the child back on the trail to a bluff overlooking the road, where she sat with little, folded hands, awaiting the coming of friends. Rescue was seemingly near, now that she had reached the great road in safety, and experience must have taught her that there would be some passing trains, if not one day, perhaps the next. It was in this situation she was seen by some soldiers, holding out her little trembling hands with joy, and calling them to deliver her.

How much of agony she must have endured as they turned away, and the fierce war-whoop of the savage rang upon her terrified soul, can never be known. Instead of the rescue and friends which, in her trusting, innocent faith, she had expected to find, fierce Indians with murderous intentions stood before her, stringing their bows to take her life—thus to win a plume to decorate a head to mark a murderer. The whizzing arrows were sent into the helpless child, and with the twang of the bowstrings a little corpse lay stretched upon the ground, and one more angel walked the golden streets of paradise, and stood before the throne of God.

The Indians, upon discovering the absence of the little girl, demanded an explanation of her absence, when, with ready presence of mind, the mother related a story, the invention of the moment, succeeding partially in allaying their suspicions. She said the child had fallen asleep, and, relinquishing her grasp of the saddle, had slipped off the horse; and that she had soon after missed her, and vainly endeavored to attract their attention to the circumstance. And having invented and told the story, she proceeded to plead that a party be sent back, and that she be allowed to accompany them, to search for the lost child; this she did to lay their suspicions. I did not doubt the truthfulness of her explanation, for it appeared to be the most reasonable, and clasped my child more closely, lest he should meet with a similar accident.

Very soon afterward we began to penetrate still more perilous places, over dizzy heights that led along the brows of black abysses: the darkness of night and the fear of the savages added terror to this perilous ride. In one of the gloomy gorges we might have taken refuge, had it not been for the vigilant eyes that were constantly upon us. The scenery around was terribly wild, and though it seemed to be impossible

for man or beast to clamber through, our captors rode
fearlessly, and the horses retained their footing with
remarkable activity. At length the sound of rippling
water convinced us of our vicinity to a river, and soon
the savages turned their horses down a steep declivity
that like a mighty wall closed in the great bed of the
North Platte.

The bluffs we had penetrated were the mountainous
hills that compelled the emigrant trains to make a detour southward. Now the broad bosom of the river
lay stretched out before us like a barrier to further progress, and, if once passed, was a line drawn between us
and the civilized world.

Lonely and pitiless everything appeared. The
twinkling stars were reflected back from the glassy surface of the water, but the moon had long since set, and
the grim shadows of the rocks looked dark and gloomy,
and the great stream seemed hastening to some known
ocean, and vexed at our intrusion upon its solitude.
Upon the sand by the edge of the water a letter was
dropped, which we hoped would be found by friendly
pursuers; and in this we were not disappointed, for it
was discovered three days subsequently and carried to
the fort, where it was recognized by my husband, and
was to him an assurance that we were being carried
away; and a gleam of hope sprang up in his breast
that, life having been spared, we might some day escape
and return; but this seeming delirium of a wounded
man's fancy was derided by more experienced persons,
who told him the accomplishment of such an under-

6

taking would be impossible without the interference of military assistance, either in battle or by ransom, and the latter was most probable of success, as it is the Indians' custom to murder prisoners on the near approach of rescuers. But still it was a relief from the terrible suspense he had suffered since our separation, and Providence seemed mercifully to have allowed it to be a messenger of assurance to him in his helpless anxiety. Though it was an old letter and had no word from us, its presence was understood.

We travelled to the northward a little by west. I endeavored to keep the points of the compass, as a knowledge of the directions we took would be of assistance if retracing the country alone. We had, when first attacked, learned that our position was fifteen miles from Fort Deer-Creek, which I supposed was, as we were, ten miles south of the Platte River.

The bluffs into which we penetrated, after crossing the river, were not as precipitous as those on the other side; yet the horses trod over dangerous places that, under calmer influences, would have caused our courage to fail at the first step; but now the great anxiety we endured seemed to consume all minor fears. Intent on saving my child and returning to my husband, I rode on with an air of resignation.

At early dawn, our way led down a precipitous bluff; and when the soft light of day was tinging the eastern sky, we emerged from the hills and entered a little valley that was covered with a luxuriant growth of grass; and through it flowed a stream of clear, cool water, spreading a delicious freshness around. Birds, awakening from their night's repose, left their perches among the boughs of the trees that grew along its banks, to sing their morning songs; and brilliantly colored flowers opened their gorgeous cups to welcome the rising sun: delicate little blossoms hid themselves among the rich shrubbery and at the roots of moss-covered trees; while long vines, suspended from the boughs, moved by a passing breeze, dipped their leaves in the sparkling brook, as it danced along, offering its refreshing influence to everything that came within its touch. The beauty and brightness of this scene seemed to mock our precarious situation, as we stood, surrounded by more than two hundred savage Indian warriors, not knowing but our lives were to be sacrificed to their caprice.

Our fate seemed too doubtful to admit of repose; and while my child lay in a troubled sleep, I sat by his side, silently praying for God's protecting mercy, and could see the hills above us dotted with Indians, stationed as pickets to give alarm in case of the appearance of approaching danger.

Our stay in this valley was about two hours, that the men might rest and the horses crop the grass along the banks of the stream.

The Indians, seeming to have no regard for properly prepared food, carry no commissaries with them in their wanderings, a superstitious idea prevailing that if they depend upon other resources than the chase, beggary, theft, and misfortunes will attend them; and, strange as it may appear, the peculiar superstition extends to mountaineers of the country, who always depend upon net and gun for food in their travels.

No breakfast was prepared, and preparations for our departure were being made, when an Indian advanced from the immediate presence of the chief, with a message from his royal highness, which was intelligibly delivered. He said it was a great distance to the Indian village, and over a dry, sandy country, interspersed with but few grassy slopes and occasional creeks, and but little timber, and it would be impossible for the child to endure the journey in safety, and most likely he would die on the way, and in consequence would become a feast for wolves; and he was now at liberty to go back.

Involuntarily my eyes fell upon the little, innocent, helpless child, who sat upon the ground before me, when the Indian — seeming to divine my thoughts, and understanding the futility of such an undertaking, well knowing, too, the inability of a child of his size to perform so great an undertaking, even if no enemies were scattered along the road — added: "He may ride a pony, which will carry him safely."

This seeming kind offer caused contending emotions, and for a while I felt unable to decide. The child urged me to allow him to go, feeling confident, in his innocent hopefulness, that he could accomplish the undertaking in safety. But opposed to my dear boy's desire and earnest feelings was the recollection of the distance we had travelled through the long

hours of the previous night, of the rocky hills, precipitous mountain-sides, dark and gloomy gorges, the
uncertainty of the points of the compass, ravenous
beasts of prey, and the mighty river; and I was convinced that the undertaking was too dangerous for a
child to accomplish, and concluded that nothing but
coercion or death should cause our separation. I
realized that this seeming authority might cause our
immediate separation or destruction, and almost fancied I saw my dear child taken from my sight forever,
and his limbs severed from the body, and the mutilated remains left upon the ground to satisfy the hungry appetite of wolves or birds of prey, when the
bones would be allowed to bleach in the sun and
storms, while his flaxen curls would be used to ornament a warrior's belt, and entitle him to the honor of
adding one more plume to his crown, as a signal that
he had, by the violence of his own hands, sent a soul
to that bourne from whence no traveller returns.

While these contending emotions were filling my
breast, the child stood silent and pale, looking hope-
fully, awaiting for me to determine. The Indian soon
returned to learn what I had concluded to do, and my
decision *must* be given. It was hard to determine, for
the fate of my only child seemed suspended in a bal-
ance, and dangers lurked in every thought, as each
moment seemed to draw him nearer to the brink of eternity. A tear stood in his eyes, and a tremor upon his
pale lips, as the awful suspense culminated. I determined to make a desperate effort to save his life, and,

6 *   E

taking his hand, I advanced a few steps toward the
savage, and explained the result of my meditation.
A frown of disappointment darkened his swarthy
brow, and his eyes fell upon his bow. No time was
to be spared — quicker than thought my child might
be beyond the power of earthly interference; and,
stepping between them, I said, "I will give the boy
to you!" and proceeded to explain the benefits that
would be derived from his services.

Frank, in his trusting hope of my superior judgment, made no resistance, though he saw that I was
relinquishing my claim as his parent, and appeared to
realize that the sacrifice on my part equalled his own.
A spirit of resignation seemed to have come over
him with the knowledge of my renewed fears, and
not a glance of reproach could be seen in his eyes,
nor a murmur escaped his lips, as he quietly bowed his
head in submission.

Placing my hand, as if by chance, upon the Indian's
strong bow, I looked into the unrelenting features of
the swarthy face with a painful anxiety that none but
a mother under similar circumstances can know, and
endeavored to detect any changing expression that
might bring hope, and assured him of my confidence
in his acceptance of my precious offering. With the
belief that the stern expression of his countenance
was softening, I proceeded to enumerate the benefits
that would be derived from Frank's assistance in the
Indian village, explaining how he could be taught to
chop wood, attend children, and bear burdens at home,

and when on the chase for game in the hills, draw the bow, and fire a gun, and dress the meat; and even on the war-path, sway the tomahawk. The savage yielded, and a pleased look lighted his features, and he almost smiled as he assured me it should be as I desired; yet to the plan of the boy laboring at home, they seemed to have a dislike — possibly because it is considered by Indians beneath the dignity of a brave to do manual labor. And now they desired me to believe that Frank was accepted as a member of the Sioux family, and was, in consequence, a young warrior by actual adoption into their tribe.

I felt persuaded, by the changed expression of the Indian's countenance, and his repeated assurances of their acceptance of the child as their own, that his life would not be immediately sacrificed, unless some competing influence should interfere and supersede this good resolution; for though the pledge was given by an enemy, whose people I was justifiable in suspecting of treachery and deceit, I believed they were given in sincerity and not to deceive; they were received in confidence, and as the only assurance that I could obtain for the preservation of the child.

I understood too little of the duplicity of the Indian character to suspect a stratagem when I was told that the child might take a horse and go back, and had only opposed our separation because of the utter inability of a boy of only seven years returning, by himself, over such a country as we had travelled, and surmounting the dangers of the way : it was a deceitful, cunning plan of the subtle chief, who had contemplated the murder of the child beyond the first bluff.

But God, in mercy, softened the warrior's heart, and caused him to admire the boy, and gain permission to spare his life.

I saw that an influence could be exerted over this savage's mind, and hoped to see in his character some of the noble traits I had been taught to believe belonged to the nature of Indians, and that, as their vigilance declined, we would meet with some opportunity by which an escape might be effected.

The chief was evidently pleased with the gift of the child; or possibly it was with the belief that I was reconciled to our life of bondage; for arrangements for our comfort were made that had not been done before: a horse was brought for me to ride, and over the saddle a heavy cloth was spread, that the seat might be as comfortable as possible. An Indian boy stooped, and, crossing his hands, motioned for me to step upon them; and, having done so, I was assisted into the saddle with as much gallantry as if the little savage had been a gentleman of refined surroundings; then, turning to the pony the chief had detailed for Frank's use, he fastened a pillow upon its back — which happened to be one from his own little bed at home — and, taking the child, he placed him upon it.

Having previously packed a third horse, and two of those faithful creatures being all of the stolen animals that had been allotted to his charge, his own included did not number enough to allow one for himself to ride. Taking our bridles, and driving the pack-horse in advance, he started up the bluff afoot.

I was forming a more favorable opinion of Indian gallantry, when he suddenly stopped and took Frank from the horse. The sight of the unexpected change in the Indian's plan gave me renewed cause for fear, and the child's pale face and imploring eyes turned toward me with a look of despair. Happily our renewed fears were but momentary, for the dexterous savage, with remarkable rapidity, grasped a little saddle, that, being too small for a comfortable seat for a man, had been abandoned, girded it upon the horse's back, and, after carefully arranging the stirrups and placing the pillow in it, he lifted the child into this comfortable seat, and again took our bridles, proceeding up the bluff; and we were soon upon a rolling prairie, where the party separated into small companies, to avoid making a single path that might lead pursuers directly upon our track. The boy continuing to walk, aroused my anxiety for his generosity, for I feared, if fatigue should overcome him, love for the child and respect for our wishes might fail him, and I requested that Frank be allowed to ride on the horse with me, while the Indian boy should ride Frank's pony; but he shook his head good-humoredly, saying, "No, no, sugar and coffee!" — intimating that it was impossible to ride the pack-horse, and that it would be unkind to incommode us by placing himself upon one of the horses that had been allotted for our use.

The way was across the country to the northwest, but by no road, though the prairie was striped with paths that had been made by the buffalo when going and returning from the hills to the creek. Each path was crossed, that if possible no track of their horses' feet might be left to mark our course.

At the camp our confiscated clothing had been in great demand, and each warrior that had been fortunate enough to possess himself of any article of our dress now arrayed himself to the best advantage the garment and his limited ideas of civilization permitted; and in some instances, when the toilet was considered complete, changes for less attractive articles of display were made with companions that had not been so fortunate as themselves in the division of the goods, that they might also share in the sport afforded by this derisive display.

Their peculiar ideas of tasteful dress rendered them grotesque in appearance. One brawny face appeared among the laces, ribbons, and artificial flowers of my straw bonnet, evincing smiles of evident satisfaction at the superiority of his decoration over his more unfortunate companions; while another was shaded from the scorching rays of the sun by a tiny parasol, and the brown hand that held it aloft was thinly covered by a black silk mitten, which was the only article of clothing, except the invariable breech-cloth, that the warrior wore.

The hand of another brave was seen vainly endeavoring to penetrate a delicate kid glove, while laces and ribbons were strewn in profusion around his neck and arms.

Vests and coats were invariably put on with the lower part upward. They all displayed remarkable fertility of imagination in their decorations. One youthful brave sported a high-crowned silk hat, and looked quite as comfortable under it as does an Eastern gentleman ; but, being derided by his more sensible companions, he threw it away in disgust, when it was immediately recaptured by a more frolicsome youth and appropriated to his own use.

The shirts, excepting the starched bosoms, were regarded as reasonable articles of clothing, and fans were used in the proper way.

They seemed to think much of their stolen goods were frivolous, and, in very many instances, worthless, decorating themselves by way of derision. One old man, however, being partially civilized, and somewhat accustomed to white men's dress, having been a frequenter at the various military stations and at French trading-posts, dressed himself, that he might make a decent appearance, with black broad-cloth pantaloons and coat, white shirt and silk vest, and black hat, all in their proper order ; and, when thus arrayed, he had very much the appearance of a civilized man, especially as he conversed in the English language; and frequently, when the others were exhibiting their ludicrous demonstrations, he assured us that no harm was intended.

It has been said that Indians are incapable of hilarity—that their laughter is but a mockery of the expression of merriment; but, opposed to this idea of the character of the forest lord, these Indians seemed to have a sensitive appreciation of the ludicrous, frequently indulging in hearty fits of laughter, and were apt in giving and receiving jokes.

It has also been affirmed that Indians do not yield to tears of sorrow, but always mourn aloud; yet observation has convinced the close observer that this is also a mistaken conclusion.

The day was excessively warm. The sand over which we travelled was scorching under the rays of the sun.

The whole country, as far as the eye could reach, was covered with artemisias and salicornias, interspersed with cactus and opuntia, and along the hill-sides occasional spots of bunch grass could be seen. Fortunately, we were not compelled to leave our heads uncovered, as is the most usual custom among these Indians. Frank wore his hat, and I a sun-bonnet. My hat had not been solicited, but its jaunty shape and trimming were too attractive in the captor's eyes to allow him to relinquish his claim unasked for. A silk mantle, that had fallen to a young Indian, was unceremoniously taken from his shoulders and exchanged for a shawl that was believed to be not as becoming for me to wear.

Though our speed did not exceed a quick walk, the journey, having been already much longer than we

were accustomed to travel on horseback, was becoming
extremely irksome, as the sun poured down its hottest
rays, scorching the ground over which we travelled,
and the country spread out before us a vast wilderness,
seeming a living grave into which we were hastening.

The pitiful face of the weary child aroused my
courage to plead for a slower pace, with the feeble hope
of being overtaken by pursuing friends; but the request was answered by the cheerless assurance that
haste was necessary to safety; for if they were closely
followed by our friends, our fate would be unquestioned, it being their duty to murder prisoners rather
than relinquish them.

7

CHAPTER VII.

ABOUT noon we arrived in a small but lovely valley, covered by a luxuriant growth of grass, through which a rippling brook ran sparkling and murmuring its song of welcome.

The camps were selected with a clear knowledge of their surroundings, and of their advantages of grass and water, which naturally suggested refreshment and repose: with a mind free from anxiety, this camp would have been a pleasant place.

Indians are very irregular in their habits of eating, surfeiting themselves when opportunity permits, and as they depend upon the precarious resources of chance and the chase in their predatory wanderings, sometimes remaining a remarkably long time before taking sustenance, but without apparent injury. Although these Indians had eaten no breakfast, dinner was not prepared; but, in the process of unrolling and admiring their plunder, several bottles of medicine were discovered, which liquid they immediately proceeded to drink; but, fearing the nauseating effect it might produce would cause them to believe they were under the

74

influence of poison, and to avenge their supposed wrong upon us, I immediately proceeded to explain to them the nature of the liquid, and they desisted.

Several glass jars filled with pickles were discovered, opened, and tasted, with indescribable contortions of countenance: after a little serious reflection, however, it was decided that cooking would be likely to improve their flavor, and a fire was immediately prepared for the purpose of trying the experiment: placing the glass jars among the flames, the plan proved to be rather startling, for very soon they burst into pieces, scattering in all directions, and letting the vinegar pour over the coals, the pickles simmering among the ashes.

This was too great an imposition for the Indians; they were disappointed and indignant. Looking contemptuously at the fragments, they exclaimed in English, "White fool, heap white fool! squaw! squaw!" and further testified their disapprobation of the result of their protection of their admired package and their cookery, by jumping around in much glee and almost frantic excitement.

We had travelled about forty miles to the northward. From our position I believed the nearest point of the Platte River to be about twenty miles, and thought Fort Dear-Creek was among the hills ten miles beyond.

During this encampment I discovered several little books that had belonged to Frank — Wilson's Series of Readers — and thought that, though in bondage, I saw a useful work for me to do. The Scriptural stories, so plainly and pleasantly told, aided the suggestion; so, attracting the attention of several of the most intelligent young men, I began to instruct them in a first lesson, and was delighted at observing the aptitude and interest they manifested, as they repeated words and listened to explanations with pleased attention, seeming to realize the necessity of being able to write, and that benefit might be derived by correspondence with their white brethren.

As a reward for my lesson in reading, they kindly offered to teach us a lesson in archery, and, placing some blunt arrows and a strong bow in our hands, endeavored to show the manner of shooting, the distance an arrow-shaft might pass into a body, etc.; but we declined. The knowledge of the use of the bow is one of the earliest teachings given to Indian boys, and sometimes even it is taught to girls; in this instance they undertook to show us both. Their conversation seemed altogether connected with shooting, cutting, scalping, and slaughtering generally.

They kept their firearms in readiness for battle, anticipating attack from our pursuing friends, and bundles of arrows were placed convenient to their hands. The points of these instruments of death are sometimes made of flint, sometimes of bone, but usually of steel, the latter being often purchased of traders who make it their business to furnish them for the Indians.

Poisoned arrows are the most deadly weapons the savages use. The poison is prepared by imprisoning a venomous snake, exciting it to attack, and then thrusting the arrow-point, previously attached to a long stick, into its mouth, at the moment the reptile ejects poisonous saliva. The arrow, thus envenomed, having once entered the flesh of a person, all hope is over. The sting is not remediable by medicine, and death is the only relief for which the unfortunate victim can hope.

Happening to discover a comb, many of them straightened their hair, and finally offered the instrument to me. Though I would have preferred my own comb, I feared to refuse theirs, and, taking the pins from my long hair, it fell loosely over my shoulders. I was proceeding to smooth it when the chief noticed it, and regarded me with a darkening and dissatisfied frown. After a few moments of gloomy hesitation, he took a great knife from his belt, whetted it, examined the edge, and, turning to his men, addressed them in a brief speech in their own language; then, approaching me, he said, "I must take your hair."

My fears had been aroused by his savage look and flourishing gestures when addressing his men, and now, as the gleaming knife neared my head, remembering he had given me no assurance of personal kindness, and that his conduct toward his men through the morning had been expressive of a very cruel nature, I had but little hope of mercy at his hands.

Frank lay sleeping by my side upon the ground: surely some blessed angel soothed his slumbers; for had he awakened and, seeing my danger, cried out, his life would have been sacrificed, or we both might

7 *

have fallen victims to the easily excited wrath of the chief. One Indian had seemed obliging, and another had been inclined to be communicative in English, and had given assurances of good will. I arose hastily, and going to the old man that could talk English, solicited his protection. He was also alarmed for my fate, and this unpleasant discovery increased my fears. Turning to their leader, he addressed him in their language, in an earnest, pleading manner, by which I understood that the chief held supreme authority over his men.

For a while the stern features retained their inflexible severity, but finally yielding under the influence of the earnest pleadings, he replaced the knife in his belt and turned away. Though it was only my hair he had intended to sever, the Indian had caused me no trifling uneasiness, and I was inexpressibly relieved by his changed manner and action. This Indian, named Tokitchey, though old, decrepit, and partially blind, was a great war-chief, holding supreme control over several bands of his tribe. His authority being unquestioned, he was zealously obeyed, though, from his inhuman disposition, he was not loved by his warriors. Sixty years of his life had been spent in rapacity and bloodshed. In his youth he had distinguished himself as the most daring warrior of his band, and, while yet a boy, won renown upon the war-path, by carrying his lance in defiance into the camp of the Crows and Shoshonees. Being promoted to war-chief for intrepid and successful conflict with the

Pawnees and other tribes, he gained honor, and his power being increased, he even faced the Comanches in hostile encounter upon the Arkansas River. During the Minnesota war he again dug up the hatchet, and, with his young braves, ravaged the border with more than usual success. His name had become a terror and a watch-cry in Indian warfare. Nor were his cruelties confined to enemies, but extended into his private life, and it was his boast that very many men had fallen by his hands, and that his teepa was ornamented by the pictures of the scalp-locks of several of his wives, who had fallen victims to jealous hatred.

It being the duty of the chief in their encampments to instruct the youth, Tokitchey, after smoking his pipe, and offering it to several others, who in turn took a whiff, proceeded to tell the following story, which was translated by the kind old man to whom reference has been made:

" When I was a boy, scarce twelve years old, I had a friend — a boy of my own age — whose parents were dead. We were sincerely attached to each other, and were companions in all our pursuits, and often rode among the hills together, sometimes for pleasure, and frequently to hunt, and often tried the speed of our animals in the valleys or upon the mountain-sides. On one occasion, when riding over a huge pile of rocks, in pursuit of a deer, my friend's pony fell, and rolled over the boy, breaking a leg and an arm of my friend. I dragged him from his painful position under the horse, and, fearing to leave him alone,

turned his pony loose, and started it in the direction
of our camp. The wounds were severe, rendering it
impossible for the boy either to walk alone or ride
my horse; and as no assistance came to us, I waited
two days, suffering, meantime, both hunger and thirst.
Then, my friend's agony becoming almost intolerable,
I started for the village, and, reaching a hill that overlooked it, I was surprised to see no traces of either
tents or people.

"I was surprised that my friends would thus forsake
me, and was considering what would be best to do,
when a party of Comanches surrounded and captured
me, taking an eastward direction. I was told that
a war-party had invaded the village, but that the people
had all fled, taking their teepas with them. The
humiliation of my position was indeed slight compared to the sufferings of my friend, as he lay alone,
looking and longing for me, whom he would never
doubt, until death relieved him from his sufferings.
How bitter must have been his disappointment, as I
failed to come! For years my dreams were haunted
by his dying groans. I imagined I saw him lying
prostrate with hunger, thirst, and his wound, and
being torn and eaten by wolves, and, as the spirit
could bear no more, turn a last look for me—and I
was not coming. This was more than I could endure.
Through cunning and watchfulness, I escaped from
my captors; but the bones of my friend I never
found. Returning to my own people, I promised the
Great Spirit to avenge my imprisonment and my dear

friend's death. Years later, when I had become a man, I sought out the people who had injured me, and, taking with me a party of my own men, we invaded their village, scattering and slaughtering all that dared offer resistance. But this did not satisfy me, and, soon after returning home, we went again; but the Comanches, having been surprised and caused to suffer by our invasion, were preparing for defence, and we dared not enter their village, but determined on a secret plundering expedition, succeeding in stealing each a young squaw. She who fell to my share was beautiful as a fawn. I loved her, and in time she became my wife, and I called her Drooping Flower. But my desire for revenge was not satisfied, and I again led an expedition to steal and murder. Among my victims was a lame man. In his flight I struck him down with my tomahawk, and scalped him while yet alive. When we had returned, telling of our daring feats, showing the scalps we had taken, Drooping Flower was sad; and though I felt brave and proud of what I had done, she refused to hold a scalp in the dance. When I demanded an explanation for her strange actions, she told me all, and I learned the story of her youth. I had slain her father, whom she loved and honored. But even this knowledge, though it grieved me for my wife's sake, gave me no remorseful pangs, for I felt an unquenchable hatred against the people who had made my home desolate and caused my beloved friend to perish alone. But when, by degrees, Drooping Flower spoke of her father, describ-

F

ing him, and telling his name and his history, I discovered the awful truth that, in endeavoring to avenge
the supposed death of my friend, I had murdered
him, and his eyes turned upon me their last look, as
I, with one sweep of my knife, severed the scalp.

"He had been found by the marauders that chased
my people and captured me, and carefully nursed.
When he recovered, remembering their kindness, and
knowing nothing of their cruelty to his 'friends, he
remained with them, and, marrying one of their
daughters, became the father of the young squaw I
had abducted and married.

"For a while the knowledge of my vengeance preyed
on my life and darkened its joys; but to mourn was
not brave.   To look upon Drooping Flower caused me
trouble, and I sent her to her mother; and, yielding
to a redoubled thirst for revenge, I drew my long knife
and bow against my neighbors; for I hated my enemies with bitterness, since they had driven me first to
desert and then to murder my friend."

This story seemed to be an index pointing to the
character of the great chief, whose commands were
religiously obeyed.   He was then the husband of eight
wives, and the father of a very large family.

CHAPTER VIII.

TWO hours were spent in this beautiful camp, when we proceeded upon the journey in a northern direction. After travelling ten miles, we again found water, and they all halted to rest a little and quench their thirst. The sun was fast sinking in the west. With a feeble hope of being overtaken by friends, I pleaded fatigue, and asked the privilege of remaining by the brook until the next morning; but my entreaties were disregarded, they having determined to proceed several miles up the valley before stopping for their night's encampment. We travelled until after dark. The third camp was in a secluded nook of the valley: it was entered at the base of a succession of bluffs and rocky peaks that almost surrounded it. Amid these encircling hills it lay, a small meadow, watered by a little brook — or possibly it was a creek of some size in other seasons of the year, but now almost dry. The enclosure was dotted by numerous bushes that were covered with green foliage.

The moon set early, and in the dim starlight could

be seen the frowning bluffs that shut us in on every side like the grim walls of a fortress. Our carriage horses were brought in, and, as I looked upon them, their familiar faces were like the countenances of dear old friends, and the thought of their services through so many years, and through our journeyings on the plains, rushed through my memory. It was the last look at those dear, faithful creatures, who, like us, were introduced to a wild, roving life.

Bushes were cut off at the ground and placed in a circular and conical form, meeting at the top, and over them coverings were stretched, making comfortable shelters, each large enough for one person to repose in. One of these little teepas, furnished with some bedding, was generously placed at my disposal; and, taking my child in my arms, I retired. Frank, being weary with his fatiguing journey, soon fell asleep. The thirty hours of our peril and privations had made sorrow painfully apparent upon his dear little face; yet, true to my injunctions, not a tear trembled in his eyes, nor a word of complaint passed his lips, nor glance of impatience darkened his brow, but quiet sorrow was impressed on every feature, while the cheerful brightness of his eyes seemed quenched when he sat in silent thoughtfulness.

I had from the first endeavored to gain the confidence of the Indians, and cause them to believe we were resigned to our fate, that, their vigilance relaxing, a chance for escape might present itself. Several small fires were made in the camp, which gave it a

cheerful appearance, and by each a guard was stationed. One being burning near the door of my little
teepa, a guard was near us. The child lay peacefully
sleeping, and I silently watching and waiting until
between midnight and morning, when, all being still,
I arose noiselessly and looked out on the scene. The
fires had burned low, and the guards appeared to
slumber, overcome, doubtless, by the fatigue of the previous day's march, and lulled to carelessness by our apparent resignation to our fate and the knowledge of the
distance we were from the fort. Softly stepping, lest
my foot should touch the slumbering form of an
Indian, I made my way to the place I thought my
friend and fellow-prisoner Mrs. Kelley lay, her bed
having been made in the open air; but, in the darkness, I could not distinguish one figure from another;
and, fearing I would be discovered if I endeavored
to search closely — remembering, too, that she had
said in the evening she would endeavor to take a horse
that night and go back, I hoped she had succeeded, and
retraced my steps to the door of my shelter.

A terrible sense of isolation overcame me. No one
can realize the sensation without in some degree expe-
riencing it. In the heart of a wilderness, a thousand
miles from home, and a prisoner in the camp of a band
of hostile savages, with but a life of slavish wanderings for myself and child, there was but one glimpse
of light in all this darkness, and that was *flight!*
But between the camp and the civilized world were
many difficulties — to pass the guards; to keep the

8

points of the compass. in the trackless wilderness; pursuers to elude; hunger and thirst to endure; possibly ravenous beasts of prey and venomous reptiles to encounter. To remain, was a life of bondage, and the companionship of barbarous Indians. I resolved to make an attempt to escape, and touching the child, he awoke, and I lifted him from the bed; fearing that he might be only partially awakened and become frightened, I whispered, "I am about starting for home;" and, clasping him closely in my arms, I looked around to discover any danger. All was quiet; not a sound, save the breathing of the sleepers, broke the silence. A few dim stars shone above the rocky peaks that surrounded us. Pressing him to my bosom in unspoken assurance of my fearless resolution to save him, I stepped noiselessly, but rapidly, across the camp to the place where we had entered it, and in precaution, instead of turning to the south by the way we had come, climbed a bluff to the westward, hoping in this way to evade pursuers.

This bluff was succeeded by another, and still others, which I climbed until my strength failed, under the laborious labor and weight of my child, and I could carry him no farther. Then, placing him upon the ground, I adjured him to run and climb for his life. He realized the necessity of doing this, and brought all his energies to the task. Thus we travelled in a southwesterly direction until morning. Judging it unsafe to travel in daylight, we sought a cañon, and concealed ourselves under the side of a projecting rock, where we remained in silent watchfulness until late in the afternoon. But, although secreted from our savage foes, who had discovered our absence at early dawn, and instituted a search which lasted until almost noon, a scarcely less terrible enemy, in the form of thirst, seized us, threatening our lives. Of hunger we had no consciousness, although it was a fast from seven meals, but water became the one absorbing thought—in it even our danger from Indians seemed forgotten. "Mother," said little Frank, as we were travelling the previous day, "I would rather go up to God than go with the Indians;" but, when his lips became parched, his throat dry, his tongue protruding so that he could scarcely speak, he said, "Mother, we might as well have been killed by the savages as to die of thirst in this cañon;" and he seemed to sink as a fading flower under the midday sun.

In childhood I had listened to my grandmother's stories of Indian cruelties, while at night my dreams had been haunted with the horrible phantoms of those recitals. To prevent my boy's brain becoming a prey to equally dreary visions, I had forbidden such narratives being related in the presence of Frank; but it was reserved for him to taste the reality of those dreadful legends, and realize the bitterness of fear I had shrunk from in description.

Crouched in the shadow of our rock of refuge, endeavoring to console the child with cheering stories and assurances that water would be at last obtained, I thought of many characters in romance and history wherein the

Indian is enshrined in beauty. The untutored nobility of soul, the brave and lofty spirit, the simple dignity, untrammelled by the ceremonies of a hollow
world, with many other traits of noble character attributed to him, rose mockingly before me, in strange contrast with the realities we had just escaped from. The
stately Logan, the fearless Philip, the invincible Te-
cumseh, the bold Black Hawk, and the gentle Poca-
hontas — how unlike the greedy, cunning, and ruthless
savages we had seen! Truly, those pictures of the children of the forest that adorn the pages of the novelist
are delightful conceptions of the airy fancy, fitted to
charm the mind — they amuse and beguile the hour.
But the true savage roams his native wastes; and to
study his real character so much must be sacrificed,
that few persons become really acquainted with him.

By some, a remarkable sagacity is attributed to the
Indian. It is even said they can discern footprints
upon a rock, and follow scents of footsteps upon the
ground; but these ideas are dreams of fancy. The
Indians cultivate the powers of the eye and the ear,
and arrive at a great degree of acuteness in those organs; which, however, might be equally the possession of any other people. Indeed, their custom of
plucking out the eyebrows and lashes, thus exposing
the pupils to sun and dust, might be supposed to be
injurious to the eyes.

Late in the afternoon, when thirst had become almost intolerable, fearing Frank's sufferings for water
would disable him for travel, his strength already fail-

ing, I concluded to go from our place of concealment and endeavor to view the face of the country; and accordingly I cautiously stepped over the sand to the base of a huge rock, and ventured to climb its craggy side until I could overlook the surrounding country; but could see no living creature. The Indian camp had been left several miles to the northeastward, and the bluffs over which we had travelled, intervening, effectually concealed the valley from view.

The surrounding country seemed a vast pile of sand, interspersed with huge rocks, productive of nothing but sage-bush and cactus — the former growing from a few inches to several feet in height, and literally covering the country for miles in extent. This herb is used by the Indians for fuel: it is somewhat like the cultivated sage, having a strong taste that resembles the flavor of that herb. Its prolific growth, however, was almost equalled in some sections by the cactus, which covered the ground for miles in extent, and its numerous formidable thorns repel intrusion wherever it spreads.

Returning to Frank, and my fears for his failing strength arousing me to the necessity of procuring water, I resolved to leave the cañon for that purpose. He was anxious to make every effort his strength would permit, and we began to climb the rocks at the side of the cañon opposite our place of entrance, with the view of leaving still another obstacle between us and the Indians' camp. Here a whip and lash were found, proving that the place had been visited before. A

8 *

little squirrel came frisking along, and, on discovering us, seemed amazed to see intruders there, and, after a few glances with its bright little eyes, whisked away among the rocks and sand from whence it came. Then a little bird alighted upon a point and fluttered about in quest of something it did not find, soon winging its way to another place, leaving the solitude to us.

We began to ascend the craggy height, and soon stood upon its summit; but the work of descending was not a trifling undertaking, and required some time and patience. When the ground was reached, we immediately started to the southeastward, with a hope of arriving at the valley we had left in the morning, a few miles south of the Indian camp. But now a painful reality interposed. When escaping from the camp, having not worn my shoes, but carrying them in my hand, hoping in this way to avoid leaving tracks in the sand, I had, in the darkness, walked into a vast bed of cactus rife with thorns, which had penetrated my feet in a painful manner. On the discovery of the pitiless thorns, I had caught the child up and carried him through, thus saving him the pain he otherwise must have suffered, and, disregarding the piercing needles, had hastened on. Possibly, it was there our pursuers were eluded, for it was not deemed probable that any person would undertake to cross an unknown bed of cactus.

Now, when I pressed my feet to the ground, the thorns caused no little pain. Frank, sympathizing

with me in this torture, begged that I would endeavor
to forget it in the recollection of the urgent necessity
of travelling, as he had found his thirst grow more
intense by dwelling upon it.

After a walk of several miles, we arrived at the
valley where we had hoped to find water; but, alas!
the stream had sunk under the surface, leaving, however, some wet mud in the bed of the creek. At the
disappointment Frank wept, for his thirst was intense;
but Heaven in mercy suggested a plan by which a few
drops of the delicious liquid might be obtained. Frank
wore two shirts: I divested him of one, and by placing
some of the moist earth in it, and pressing it with my
hands, a few drops of water were obtained, which fell,
like pearls, into the mouth of the child. It was a
most welcome draught, though muddy, and much
impregnated with iron. It brought back the life that
seemed ebbing under the torture of thirst. According
to the geographical account of the country, this was
probably the head of Sage Creek. Abundance of tall
grass grew in the valley, and a few rose-bushes were
scattered upon little knolls that dotted it, and though
the season for roses was almost over, a few were left
blooming. We followed the stream, or rather the valley, for one or two miles, and could see the prints of
footsteps of birds in the moist earth, as they too had
searched for water.

Nothing of animal life was seen, except a deer, that
leaped from its covert at our approach, and escaped
over the hills.

Finally we came to a little pool of water that tenaciously held its position in the bed of the creek. Its surface was covered by a green scum, and innumerable little snakes darted about on seeing us approach, and seemed, by their hasty movements of swimming from shore to shore, lapping their slender tongues, darting keen glances from their gleaming little eyes, to resent our approach. We, however, were persevering, and, in spite of their hostile demonstrations and hurried movements, advanced to the brink, and stooped to drink of the tempting liquid; first, however, taking the precaution of frightening the reptiles away, and spreading a cloth upon the surface; and we only drank of what strained through, lest we might swallow some tiny reptiles.

Farther down the valley more water was found. But soon the creek, with its lovely green, turned to the eastward, and we were compelled to leave it and pursue our way southward, over the dry and desolate hills.

The sun was fast sinking behind the western peaks, and we only awaited the friendly shadows of night to pursue our way over the wild and arid heights before us, not daring to venture in daylight, lest the watchful eye of a wary savage should detect our movements. Having procured some moist earth in a cloth for its dampness, in case no water could be found on the road, we treasured it as a preserver of life.

While sitting in a sheltered retreat, awaiting the sun's decline, we observed, to the northward, a small

party of Indians advancing, but apparently unconscious of our presence in the vicinity. They were at
a distance of several hundred yards, and were not
recognized as being of the party we had escaped from.
Our only safety was in concealment. Cautiously we
crept to some large bunches of sage-bush, and were
shielded by their protecting leaves. Yet painful suspense was endured, as the savages approached and
passed within a few yards of us.

As night spread her sable mantle over the hills, bringing coolness and repose to the weary, the young moon
shone faintly, and a few stars could be seen ; but silence
reigned : not even a sound of the murmur of water or
hum of insects could be heard upon the clear air. I
arose, and felt in the darkness for the child. He slept
where last I saw him. It was cruel to disturb that
needed rest, yet many miles of weary walking lay
between us and our own people. With a silent prayer
to God for protection, I awoke him, and we proceeded
upon the journey.

As we ascended the hills the wind arose, blowing
fresh and cold. We continued to walk all night, looking stealthily on every side for the approach of danger,
and expecting at any moment we might overtake the
band that had passed us in the evening, in their night
encampment. Just before daybreak the darkness was
intense, and the way so rugged that it was deemed
advisable to wait until morning, which would give a
view of our surroundings. Accordingly we went
aside a few steps to seek a hiding-place beneath the

shelter of some sage-bush. Soon the weary child fell
asleep, but the intense anxiety for water prevented me
from finding rest. We had seen no signs of water
since we left Sage Creek, and it might yet be days
before it could be obtained.

The horrors of our situation were harassing to contemplate, and once a thought of returning to the pool
we had left presented itself; but reason coming to aid
a better resolution, the cowardly suggestion was ban-
ished, and, as the first rays of daylight tinged the
eastern horizon, I arose to look upon the surrounding
country. The wolves seemed congregated upon the
highlands, and, awaking from their night's repose,
their wailing cries echoed back from the distant hills
with terrific clearness.

These prowling creatures abound in that country,
where some species attain a great size. They congre-
gate in large numbers, attacking the stray animals they
happen to meet. Even the buffalo, which does not
fear them in the herd, knows his danger when overtaken alone; and the solitary bull, secreted from its
hunter, succumbs before the united force of a gang of
wolves.

Advantage is sometimes taken of the unsuspecting
buffalo by the Indian, who covers himself with a wolf-
skin, and creeping cautiously, is permitted to approach
within a few yards of the herd, when he is able to
discharge his arrows with deadly effect. In this way
great slaughter is sometimes made by the cunning
savages. Each secures a piece of meat for present use,

leaving the carcass to become a feast for wolves — thus wasting their own game.

When the day became clear, a green valley could be seen to the southward, and, dreading the agony of thirst Frank might suffer, I concluded to mark the place, and proceed in search of water alone. Being soon convinced that the hope was not delusive, and that it really could be obtained, I returned for Frank, and, to my horror, could not find the spot where I had left him. The direction was not lost, but, in my eagerness, I had travelled farther than I had anticipated. For a while I searched with anxious dread, with frantic ardor hastening through the sage-bushes; but a great sameness prevailed, each place appearing much like another.

At length he awoke, and, finding himself alone, stood up and cried. My joy was great, for truly " the lost was found." Together we hastened into the valley, and on the way thither came into a deserted Indian camp, and from its relics selected a pair of abandoned moccasins, which, being bound upon Frank's bruised and bleeding feet, served as a shield to protect them from the scorching sand. Farther in the valley, covered with a luxuriant growth of grass, we found a creek flowing over a bed of unusually white sand. This water was very cold, and though of the depth of two feet, was so clear that it appeared to be but a mere ripple above the sand.

This section was evidently a great Indian rendezvous, and, lest we be observed, it was necessary to seek a secluded place in which to spend the day. Looking about, we discovered the mouth of a small creek that emptied into this stream from the south-west. Thither we went, and found the waters, though occupying so nearly the same section of country, to be in great contrast with the first creek — one being of icy coldness and clear as crystal; the other warm and stagnant, and of a greenish color.

With the conviction that Indians would probably make their encampments near the best water and most luxuriant grass, we selected our secluded retreat for the day near the other.

This temporary home was a cavity in the side of a bluff, rising perpendicularly from the valley at the southward. It had been formed by the action of water that flowed from the hills into the valley in wet seasons. It was of oval shape, and about thirty feet in length, with perpendicular walls on either side, which were about twenty feet high and twelve feet apart.

The mouth was a narrow passage, which had been formed by the outward flow of the water through a rock; and in this natural doorway grew clusters of wild rose-bushes, which concealed the entrance from view; and just beyond the door was a pool of water that, like a good fairy, promised to keep away the bane of thirst. This was a tolerably safe retreat, if our tracks should not be discovered and guide the savages to our seclusion.

The sun arose in all its majestic beauty — not a cloud

intervened to obscure the golden rays, as they tinged the tops of lofty peaks and nestled into silent nooks, thus overspreading the vast arid hills. Not even a bird was seen to soar or flit upward, and but the murmur of the sparkling brook broke the silence of that long and ever-to-be-remembered day.

The pool of water near our door was of a green color, and inhabited by slender dark-colored reptiles, which very much resembled horse's hairs, and were supposed to be tiny roots, until a closer observation revealed the truth that instead of floating by the action of the water they possessed animal life, and had eyes, and, looking at us, curved their slender forms, seeming to resent our approach.

They were about twelve inches in length, and not much, if any, greater in circumference than a hair from a horse's mane; but on close observation one end was discovered to be larger, about the size of the head of two common pins, and their little eyes to glisten beneath the waters.

9   G

CHAPTER IX.

A SCANT MEAL — A DISCOVERY — BEAUTIFUL EFFECT OF THE
MIRAGE UPON THE SCENERY — ARRIVAL IN SIGHT OF THE
PLATTE — GRAND SCENERY — JOYFUL DISCOVERY OF
FRIENDS — BURIAL OF LITTLE MARY.

LOOKING about in hope of finding a rose-bud,
an empty egg-shell was discovered, from which
the little warbler had winged its flight, and upon this
we dined. It proved to be the only meal that broke
our fast of four days.

Later in the day, when on a cautious visit to the
neighboring pool, we discovered a very large toad
sitting in the grass, pouting silently, as though pon-
dering over some great wrong. Frogs are eaten by
civilized people, but toads never; nor will Indians
use them for food. Their appearance is repulsive and
disagreeable to such an extent as to lead to the belief
that they are a poisonous reptile; yet it has been said
that some soldiers, during the Revolutionary war, in
great extremity, ate them.

This toad we captured and carried triumphantly to
our cave; and we resolved that, whatever its exterior
homeliness might be, it should serve as a shield against
a day of starvation. To kill it without a weapon was
now a matter of consideration; and finally a little stick

was procured and used vigorously; but the reptile clung
tenaciously to life, and only yielded under repeated
blows. It finally lay dead upon its breast. The
dressing now became a matter of no little difficulty, as
the loathsome appearance forbade the touch of the hand.
With the aid of the stick, however, the undertaking was finally accomplished, as the skin was only
attached to the body at the lips and toes, and when it
was thrown out of sight, if it had not been for the
great force of unpleasing associations attached, the
flesh would have seemed as delicate as the breast of a
little bird; yet we refrained from eating it, reserving
it for a greater emergency, our prejudices not being
easily overcome. It is said these creatures undress
themselves at certain seasons of the year, and, viewed
by an observer, seem to disrobe after the fashion of
men — first drawing out one limb and then the other,
and in like manner divesting themselves of the
sleeves. When the operation is completed, the little
fellow suddenly presents himself in a new suit of
brown. Perhaps the time had arrived for our toad to
assume new apparel, and that was possibly the reason
it was easily divested of the old.

Some rose-leaves and the small game were secured
in our pockets, and at night some moist earth was
placed in a cloth, for it might be a refreshing balm in
the absence of water. Slowly the sun went down;
and night hovered over the hills as we resumed our
journey. More hills were to be climbed. Soon we
discovered that the mud we carried in the cloth would

not retain moisture, and, in consequence, was worthless.   We had now been long fasting, and the absence
of food aggravated thirst.

The country was high and barren, and no signs of
water being discovered, a fear that none could be obtained haunted us as night wore on.   At length the
child's strength failed to such a degree that he could
walk but a few steps in succession, and must rest a
little.   He begged to be permitted to lie down, but I
knew it would be unsafe to travel in daylight, and,
fearing Frank would not survive the next day unless
water be procured, I endeavored to encourage him
onward — reminding him of the weary hours of the
previous night; how we had travelled over sandy
heights and dreary wastes to find at morning dawn
water and rest.   Now the night was far spent, and
soon a new day would come, when we would probably
be as fortunate as before.   A large white flower
nodded gracefully on its slender stalk, and seemed a
reminder of the poppy in the garden of our Pennsylvania home.   Its dwelling-place was among the
mountains, where it stood blooming alone, seeming,
by its contentment and beauty, to mock our strivings.
I plucked it for its moisture and fragrance, and offered
it to Frank, but he declined it, remarking, "I do not
care for flowers now;" and, trembling under the influence of fatigue, hunger, and thirst, his husky voice
and pleading eyes again begged for rest.   I was unable
to carry him, and could but realize the painful truth
that his strength was exhausted.   I sought a small

wash in the ground, and, taking him in my arms, lay
down and fell asleep.   Soon the day dawned, when the
shrill voices of the wolves rang upon the clear morning
air, rousing us to a sense of immediate danger.

A little sleep had revived the child somewhat.
We arose, and, contrary to our previous intentions,
began to travel in daylight.   The danger being divided,
and it being scarcely less terrible to risk the withering
influence of thirst and the attack of ferocious wolves
in our seclusion than the savages in travel — the former
evil was almost certain — and as our way was not to
the place of our attack, which the Indians would most
likely suspect, we hoped to elude the latter, and proceeded on our lonely walk.

It was not exclusively a time of suffering; for
though cast out, as it were, from the world, there
was magnificent scenery to enjoy.   A grand panorama
spread in majestic beauty before us; yet not as splendid as is that sometimes seen in this mountainous
country, where the most sublime objects in nature
are crowded into a scene as wild and beautiful as
imagination can picture.   The rarity of the atmosphere, nowhere more inviting than on the vast slopes
and plateaus of the Rocky Mountains, gives to every
thing a mystic beauty.   Small objects close at hand
start up with remarkable rapidity into gigantic mon-
sters.   A raven, at a short distance, looks like some
large animal, and when the deception is discovered,
recalls to mind the monster birds described by Sinbad
the Sailor; and far-off buttes mock, with their retreat-
9 *

ings, the approach of the traveller, who, thinking that a few moments' ride will bring him to a landmark, a pool of fresh water, or some approaching stranger, travels onward, while the visions sink one by one behind the horizon, above which refraction has raised them. Sometimes a solitary antelope, walking alone, will be multiplied into a band of twenty, and a small herd of seven or eight look like the march of a band of Indians, causing fears lest it be pursuing savages. Sometimes the artemisia patches, rocks, and alkaline flats, covered with the incrustation of alkali sparkling in the sun, suddenly seem to vibrate before the eyes and transform themselves into lakes and gardens of most bewildering beauty; then, with a misty vapor, pass away, leaving the barren plain in its blank sterility as before — a desolation covered with artemisia or buffalo-sage, and prickly pear, patches that add little beauty to the surrounding desolation.

Still, over the desert-like wilderness, the antelope roams in vast numbers, and the huge bison flounders in comparative security. Sailing in mystic curves, the American eagle surveys the plains, unconscious of danger, or swoops with fearful rapidity upon the unsuspecting rabbit or sage-hen, and bears it to his eyry with a triumphant scream.

About nine o'clock we descended to the bed of a creek or shallow river, whose waters had all disappeared beneath the sand, or under the influence of evaporation, as is not uncommon in that country in dry seasons.

A green tree could be seen down the stream, standing like a forest-king, spreading its branches to the
weary traveller of the desolate hills.   When we had
crossed this sandy creek and gained the opposite bluff,
great smoky hills could be seen to the southward,
looming up against the morning sky, adding their wild
grandeur to the surrounding scene.   Soon a green valley of thirty miles' width spread out before us, and
through it rolled a mighty river, whose windings amid
verdant banks could be marked from our elevation, and
the emerald spots of luxuriant green that dotted the sil-
very crest were visible upon its bosom, while the rays
of the July sun were reflected back from its glassy surface in dazzling splendor.

Those hills were a spur of the Rocky Mountains,
and are said to derive their smoky appearance from
the burning of bituminous coal, in which they abound.
The great river was the North Platte, and, although
miles of weary walking lay between us and its cool
waves, and, even when gained, it might be too much
swollen to ford, the prospect of relief from thirst, and
the consciousness of being thus far on our homeward
journey, brought renewed hope.   The road lay over
great, sandy hills, and the scorching sun seemed to
wither all vegetation under its influence.

Frank's hat and my bonnet were left behind, and
our heads were exposed to the hot rays of the sun.   I
had undertaken to make temporary caps, but, being
warned by Frank that white could be seen at a great
distance, and might lead to discovery just when hope

had sprung into our hearts, I desisted, thankfully accepting his suggestion.

On ascending another eminence, what appeared to be an Indian village, resting upon the opposite bank of the river, presented itself in bold relief, and to the eastward, at the distance of a few miles, another village was located between us and the river, as if guarding the blessed refreshing liquid.

It was death to retrace our steps, and dangerous to go forward; one moment in that exposed place might cost us our lives or a recapture. Our position was on the brink of a precipice, and at its base could be seen a clear pool or lake that had formed from the super-abundance of the river, but was beyond our reach, over two hundred feet below, while its cool and tempting freshness only increased the desire to be at its brink. There was but one thought, which came like a flash — safety; and a moment later we were concealed from the danger amid the gaping walls of a cañon's mouth, that opened immediately at our right, as if to offer a shelter that otherwise we could not have found. It was entered by a gradually descending slope for a few feet, and then a narrow passage between two rocks seemed to open for us to pass, and down into its cool declivity we went. Strong and high the massive rocks rose above us, and we seemed buried alive in the bowels of the earth.

Nothing grander than this mighty cañon did my eyes ever rest upon, and feeble words can convey but a faint impression of the wondrous beauty of this noble

feat of nature.   After reaching a gentle slope, we came
to a steep descent of stones, resembling stair-steps,
without the aid of which it would have been impossible to penetrate its depths.   The greater space below,
when gained, resembled the cell of some old prison ;
and in it we felt more severed from the breathing, thinking world.   Passing still farther down this cañon, for
it was long and seemingly divided into rooms or apart-
ments, we came to a natural hall, paved with smooth
rock, and overhung with arched walls, gray and rough,
and garnished with curious devices.   Beautiful white
stones, of various shapes and sizes, decorated the place,
being disposed around in grotesque shapes and exquisite harmony of order. ·

Even weariness, fear, and thirst did not deaden the
faculties beyond the power of enjoying this masterpiece
of nature's cunning workmanship, on which she had lav-
ished so much skilful tracery, to rear a palace for the
abode of silence, for not a sound broke the quiet, whose
solemn presence was felt, if not seen.   The way led
over rocks, and cautiously we went across places that
our feet were the first to press.

Penetrating still farther into this wonderful museum
of the great mother's art, among rocky walls, whose
faces appeared chiselled by the hand of man into
images of ancient gods in bas-relief, at another turn
the scene changed, and we would start to behold ourselves in the midst of some dim cathedral aisle, and
it would have required but a slight effort of the imagination, in the uncertain light, to supply the arched

roof with carved fretwork and Gothic ornaments, and add figures of saints to the shadowy gloom.

Every passage assumed a distinct character, equally curious, if not more fantastic, than the one preceding it, and each impressed its reality so clearly on our wondering eyes that we might almost have suspected an approaching Indian of being a creature of some mysterious life and power.

Resting where the way seemed too perilous to penetrate, until courage and accustomed sight robbed it of some of its terrors — then creeping on stealthily, and always urged forward by thirst and hope of the goal to be won at the end of the race, suddenly we came to a projecting rock that overhung a dark bed below, and here, in the sombre light, we sat down, for the obstruction seemed too great to be surmounted.

It was now twenty-two hours since we had tasted water, and we seemed to sink under the influence of thirst. The way had been over a dry, sandy waste that was scorching under the sun. Now the cooling shades of the towering walls on either side were as a refreshing balm, but could not supply the need of water; and that became the one absorbing thought. Water in the river; water in the well; water at the fount; water in the lake; water everywhere!

After resting awhile, a descending slope was discovered, and we proceeded. We soon came to where the floor was of sand, and a great tree presented itself in bold relief, but appeared, in its prison walls, as a tree of insignificant growth. At this place the sand was damp, and immediately at the right was the mouth of another mighty cañon, which, with a hope of finding water, we entered, and though this new wonder presented fearful forebodings, it also gave hope. We hurried onward, inspired with a growing certainty that water would be found, and soon came to a pool of bright, clear, cold water — the best of liquids. During that night and day it had seemed that if once it was within our grasp, our thirst would be insatiable — never tiring of the refreshing stream; but the delusion of the thought was soon discovered.

It was more than one hundred hours since we had eaten food, yet we were not conscious of a desire for it.

This cañon was in great contrast with its sister we had just visited, every thing being damp. The sand beneath our feet was moist; great pools of water stood here and there, and occasionally a stream rippled along and then sank in the porous strata of sand, to rise again in pools, or to flow along at the base of the mighty walls and mingle with drops that dripped from their sides. Pale flowers, that had never been kissed by a ray of sunshine, drooped their delicate heads among the mountain-moss, to sip the little drops that fell in soft spray upon its bosom. Long vines dangled under a load of water, but had never been fanned by a passing breeze; a dewy moisture pervaded the air. This cañon, though not so grotesque, was truly beautiful, and in it were marks of former intrusion.

A boot-track and a print of a horse-shoe were dis-

covered in the sand. Savages do not wear boots, nor
are their horses shod. A hope — not a delusive hope
— sprang to our breasts. We had previously heard
the tinkling of a bell and the lowing of a cow, but
had supposed they belonged to the Indians of the
neighboring village; but now it seemed a proof, in
connection with the tracks, that possibly civilized people were in the vicinity. Hastening back to the dry
cañon, I ascended the side and looked eagerly for
any assurance of the vicinity of a civilized person.
Again the lowing of a cow, as pleasant music, broke
the silence, for it carried with it hope. Indians only
steal cattle for their meat. We felt that we *must* be
near the camp of Christian people.

Hastening to Frank, I took his hand and ascended
the opposite side, which, since the junction of the
cañons, was a huge embankment of sand; even roots
and bushes were interspersed.

Freshly chopped wood was found upon the side.
There a hunter had been. I left the child, believing
the mark sufficient to secure my finding him again;
and climbing still higher, I caught a glimpse of the
valley we had so long been approaching.

Knowing our danger from the savages that roam
the hills, every possible assurance that civilized people
were really in the neighborhood was necessary, lest,
with a delusive thought, we might rush into danger.

A cloud of dust arose beyond the river, and sailed
along as though it was being raised by a little whirl-
wind from a public highway. The village could be

seen, but it was at too great a distance for the people to be recognized as Indians.

The lowing of cows, the tinkling bell, the tracks in the sand, cut wood, the dust as of a highway, all rose up as evidences of a vicinity to white people. Possibly a train was encamped near the Indian village. Perhaps we were nearing the emigrant road, and much nearer the fort than had been supposed. Calculating the distance we had been taken by the Indians, and the way we had come in returning, we had not hoped to strike a frequented road for ten miles beyond the Platte River; but now, the cheering evidences of our vicinity to civilized life combined, formed an illuminating light, such as had not shone before in our saddened minds, and just as the last ray of the glorious sunset died on the tops of the surrounding hills, the clear, soft sound of music floated through the still air and lingered upon the rocks to echo back the enrapturing notes; and at that moment, an eagle, with wide-spread wings, sailed proudly aloft into the dying sunset.

At the sight of the noble bird and the sound of our nation's horn, danger seemed to fly, and I bounded down the rocky steep to carry the good tidings to my son. He, too, had caught the sound, and, with hope and joy beaming in his eyes, exclaimed: "The soldiers, ma! I hear the bugle sound retreat."

It was truly so; and, clasping my dear child in my arms, we rejoiced together.

Having bathed and combed at the pool, no future

10

preparations were to be made to complete our restricted toilet, and we proceeded to the mouth of the united cañons by a passage between two precipitous bluffs that led several hundred feet downward to the river.

Leaving these strange monuments of nature's work forever, I must say one word more.

Their extent appeared, in my limited investigation, to be terminable; yet we felt that we had scarcely passed the threshold of the damp one, though it might end abruptly even when the vista seemed to lead on to new wonders. Their entrance is so insignificant as to be overlooked by strangers, and had hitherto escaped the traveller's attention; though a mountaineer, whose track we had seen, had, in pursuit of a bear, penetrated a little distance, but, being persuaded that the gloom was too intense, he retreated.

Arriving on the bank of the stream under the cover of night, we sought the shelter of some bushes, for the mighty river rolled between us and the fort. The village we had seen on the north side was some little distance below us, and we still believed it to be inhabited by savages who would capture or murder us immediately on discovery. Caution had been learned through bitter experience; and, although there were so many evidences of our vicinity to a friendly settlement, we dreaded lest a lurking savage, discovering us at the threshold of friends—for we felt that we were surely approaching the place of a white man—we still cautiously avoided exploring a path that might be beset with dangers.

As we sat in this shelter, which proved to be the last, a most joyful and welcome sound greeted our ears — one in which there was no mistake — our own language, spoken by some boys who passed, driving cattle.

We arose at the pleasant and encouraging sound and the sight of the boys, and, believing that what we had supposed was an Indian village might be an emigrant train, walked slowly in that direction, and soon saw a man who was approaching with two horses, and called to him. He came forward, and I inquired if he was a white emigrant, when he proudly raised his head and said, "Well, I believe I am." Then I endeavored to explain to him why I thus unceremoniously addressed him, but he interrupted me by saying, "Oh, yes, I already have heard of the Indians' outbreak, and that you were carried away; but no one ever dreamed of your coming back by yourself. Two companies of soldiers have arrived at Deer Creek, just beyond the river, on their way to chastise the red scoundrels. But, come along with me, and I will take you to the train, where there are ladies." And, still holding my hand, he drew us with him.

"As you are acquainted with the circumstances, can you tell me where the men of the train are?" I inquired. "Your husband," he replied, "was wounded, but not fatally, and is beyond the river, in the fort." This was the first intimation I had that any of our train had been shot when the Indians fired; and, in hope that some mistake existed, I made further inquiries; but the kind man knew the truth, and having heard of a little boy being carried away, and seeing Frank, knew it was my husband that was convalescent, and proceeded to explain.

We soon arrived at the place where the women were, and were introduced and cordially welcomed. Never before was I so glad to see ladies. They were, of course, all strangers to me, but, notwithstanding, they seemed as sisters; while some laughed, others cried, each in her way expressing joy at our return. Their interest and sympathy were like healing balm after our dreary wanderings among the hills. It was regarded as but little less than a miracle that we had made our escape from the savages, entirely unaided, and successfully found our way back. Very soon hundreds of persons flocked to see us and inquire in what manner we had effected an escape, and how we found our way back to that point, etc., etc.

Many of these good people were Germans, and, as they conversed among themselves, expressed a very great hatred to the Indians. I felt almost persuaded that they were as much imbittered against the savages as myself.

For an hour this entertainment lasted, and, though I felt weary and faint, I endeavored to reply correctly to all their questions, although it seemed one unceasing stream of inquiries.

This train had come from Iowa, and the river being very high, they had been unable to cross until they arrived at that place, and were awaiting a fall in the water. Numerous small trains coming up, the encampment was increased to a great size; and, upon first sight, the covered wagons. appeared like an Indian village. Thus arose my first impression that it was a savage camp. With great kindness a sumptuous supper was prepared, but, although our fast had been long, we felt no desire for food, and I declined to accept anything but a cup of tea and a small piece of bread, and permitted Frank to have only a little milk and rice, at the taste of which his appetite returned; but mine did not, until tempted by delicacies prepared by kind ladies at the fort, on the second day after our arrival.

As the waters were too high for us to cross that night,. a soldier, by the name of Sparks, who happened to be there, kindly offered to cross the river and inform my husband of our safe arrival, when Mr. Kelley immediately came over to inquire the fate of his family, but I was able to give him no very encouraging information.

The afflicted husband and father's emotion, on listening to what I could tell, was a sight that moved strong hearts — his wife, still in captivity, with all the horrors of uncertainty surrounding her, and his little daughter alone upon the hills, or carried away by another party, or, perhaps, mutilated and left for wolves to prey upon. All this seemed to press heavily upon his mind and feelings. Endurance struggled with stronger sentiment; but the great sorrow that oppressed his heart did not prevent him from sympa-

10 *   H

thizing with our joy; and he related the particulars
of the condition of the wounded, and assured me
that my husband was convalescent. Avowing his own
intention to start the next morning in search of his
lost child, he returned to the fort and the bedside of
the wounded men. In accordance with his plan, Mr.
Kelley procured a squad of men, it being unsafe to
go alone, and proceeded in search of the lost child.
It was now six days since she had been left by herself.
The squad of soldiers, in their search, came up to a
company of emigrants standing a little back from the
road; but, alas, too late! The body of little Mary
had been found pierced by three arrows, and she had
been scalped by the ruthless knife; but whose guilty
hands shed her innocent blood we can never know,
since no friendly eye beheld her after she was seen by
the terrified soldiers sitting upon a bluff. When discovered by a traveller, her body lay with its little
hands stretched out, as if she had received, while
running, the piercing, deadly arrow.

None but God knew the agony of that young heart
in its terrible extremity, and surely He, who numbers
the sparrows and feeds the ravens, was not unmindful
of her in that awful hour, but allowed the heavenly
kingdom, to which her trembling soul was about to take
flight, to sweeten, with a glimpse of its beatific glory, the
bitterness of death — even as the martyr Stephen, seeing the bliss above, could not be conscious of the torture below.

To the travellers, who found her, she was only the

mutilated corpse of a murdered child. They could not guess her name or people, but with humane feelings gave her a resting-place in the earth, and, with the usual precaution in such cases, secured a piece of her dress by which the body might possibly be identified. When these duties were over, and the sorrowing father had the sad satisfaction of smoothing the earth upon the unconscious breast that had ceased to suffer or be afraid, and to know that his task was done, there they left her in the wilderness — a little grave all alone, far from the happy home of her childhood and the sisters and brothers among whom she had played in innocent joy.

Of all strange and terrible fates, no one, who had seen her gentle little face in its loving sweetness, the joy and comfort of her adopted parents' hearts, would ever have predicted such a barbarous one for her. But it was only the passage from death into life, from darkness into daylight, from doubt and fear into love and endless joy. Those little ones, whose spirits float upward from their downy pillows, amid the tears and prayers of broken-hearted friends, are blest to enter in at heaven's shining gate, which lies as near little Mary's rocky, blood-stained pillow in the desolate waste as the palace of a king; and when she had once gained the great and unspeakable bliss of heaven, it must have blotted out the remembrance of the pain that won it, and made no price too great for such delight.

CHAPTER X.

IT was the 17th of July, and five days since our capture, that we crossed the broad bosom of the North Platte, on our way to Fort Deer-Creek. The waters had fallen so as to allow us to go over in a wagon, and, as the ripples rose around the horses' plunging feet, it brought the recollection of the time we crossed compulsorily under the command of Indian guides. Then each wave seemed to rise to shut out hope of return, and the wide waters, when we gained the opposite side, lay like an impassable barrier between us and friends.

Through our journey back, this river had been a mountain of difficulty to our minds; I realized it must be crossed, but how its deceitful quicksands and changing channel would be overcome had cost much contriving thought. At last I had determined to wait upon the bank, or secluded among the hills, until the water should reach only to my shoulders, and then, with the child on my arm, endeavor to cross by ford-ing. The depth could be ascertained by wading in, and at each experiment, when the water was too deep, return and wait until it appeared less formidable, and so by patient, untiring effort, finally reach the opposite side.

That was my plan, but Heaven in mercy sent an easier crossing, among friends who, though yester-day strangers, were already much interested in our welfare.

My husband was prostrated by loss of blood and the effects of his wound, and the news of our return had been so unexpected that he could scarcely realize our safety until he saw us by his side.

Though we fervently thanked God for our deliv-erance from captivity and from the dangers through which we had passed, it was impossible to avoid de-pression when we thought of our hapless situation, reduced to poverty in that far-distant and peculiarly barren country, and my husband without health to commence anew.

Realizing our forlorn condition, little Frank, with tears in his eyes, said, "Mother, I suppose now I shall never be able to get an education."

I installed myself as my husband's nurse, and our unfortunate friend, Mr. Wakefield, too, lay suffering with wounds which afterward proved fatal, though he survived eight months.

Two weeks previous to our capture we had caused

Frank to be vaccinated, and the pits were still visible upon his arms and neck, yet I had entirely forgotten the circumstance; but the quick eye of the doctor detecting the traces of the marks, pronounced them small-pox, and ordered our tent to be detached from the fort to prevent contagion. Believing that it was the bite of ants, which in our travels seemed everywhere present, I endeavored to persuade him to that conclusion, but in vain; and only the commandant's disregard of his order prevented the wounded from being moved to another locality.

My fears while in the fort were not entirely at rest, for a number of teepas inhabited by squaws and Indian children were in the garrison, and it was these, together with the soldiers' tents, I had mistaken for an Indian village beyond the river, when we were upon the bluffs.

The Indians were now considered extremely hostile all over the country, and no one ventured beyond the limits of the reservation alone, as savages could be seen lurking among the hills. They had even been so bold as to undertake to drive off the Government herd, and the attacking of emigrant trains was now of every-day occurrence.

The morning after our arrival at the fort, some squaws were observed beyond the enclosure, signalling as though something was to be communicated. A general fear of the savages prevailed, and no one desired a lonely ramble from the fort; and to prevent venturesome travellers risking too much, a military order, forbidding trains from leaving the vicinity without a certain number of armed men, was issued by the district commandant.

Immediately after the report of the attack of the train had reached Fort Deer-Creek, Colonel Collins, commandant of the military district, ordered two companies, under command of Captain Shoeman and Captain Marshall, two brave and daring gentlemen, to pursue, and rescue the prisoners, and chastise the savages in case of resistance. But the distance of one hundred miles lay between those two forts, and they only arrived at Fort Deer-Creek, on their way in pursuit of the offenders, the evening we returned; but as there was still one prisoner out, the second morning they resumed their march in pursuit of the marauders, and after an absence of three days returned, but had not been successful.

Alas! misfortune had attended the expedition in the loss of a young and daring officer, Lieutenant Brown, of the 11th Ohio Volunteers, who, with a small squad of men, left the main body to prospect the neighboring hills in quest of the enemy. Coming suddenly upon a band of warriors in their encampment, the lieutenant, rather indiscreetly, ordered an attack; but his men, seeing the futility of opposing such numbers, fled, leaving the officer by himself. Becoming conscious of his dangerous situation, he feigned friendship, addressing them in the usual way: "*How coola?*" But they were not thus to be deceived, and sent a well-aimed arrow that penetrated his neck, and he fell from his horse.

He was reported dead, and with all the speed our men could command they pursued his murderers; but the fresher horses of the savages carried them off beyond their reach, and the soldiers were compelled to return in disappointment. Stopping to procure the body of the fallen officer, it was discovered that he still lived, and as they approached he murmured, "Water!"

His murderers had divested him of his clothes. He had lain eight hours in the sun, with the arrow between the pharynx and the cervical vertebra, in dangerous proximity to the carotid artery. Being left alone, and conscious of his situation, it is difficult to depict the agony he must have suffered. He was removed to camp, where the arrow was extracted, and he died. His remains were taken to Fort Deer-Creek for interment, and thence to his friends in Ohio.

The commandant of Fort Deer-Creek, Captain Ryn-heart, had married an Indian woman, who resided with him in the fort. This tawny wife was not beautiful, nor was she amiable, judging from the fearful outbreaks of temper in which she indulged. During her paroxysm of passion she would come bounding toward him, with a knife in her hand, declaring she would cut him into pieces; but generally he could succeed in coaxing her into a good humor. If mild means failed he would threaten to drive her from his lodge forever, which seemed to be harsh treatment for a husband to his wife; but, as it was the only available means within his power, and only used to quell her wrath, having sufficient effect to calm her stormy temper, he appeared justifiable.

This unfortunate officer was put under arrest for some minor offence; but was temporarily released, on account of the scarcity of officers. One night, going with a squad of men to reconnoitre for Indians, supposed to be hostile and lurking in the neighborhood, coming upon some lodges among the hills, he dismounted, and ordered his men to shoot the first man that came from a lodge. He then entered, and discovering the occupants to be of the friendly Indians, and they recognizing him as an officer and the husband of a daughter of their people, he made a friendly visit, his men remaining without; but no sooner did he leave the tent than a bullet entered his heart, in obedience to his last command.

His remains were taken to Ohio, to his friends. His Indian wife grieved sorely and loudly, cutting gashes in her flesh and weeping bitterly; as did her female friends. Soon afterward she became the mother of a son, an unfortunate little boy, whose destiny was fixed for the mountains.

Some very kind and sympathizing ladies of Fort Laramie believed it to be the duty of Mrs. Rynheart, the lawful wife, who was at home, to send for and adopt the Indian woman's child, through respect to her husband.

Many white men live among these hills, having

11

Indian families. They are chiefly Canadian French; but there are some exceptions in favor of our nation. Some of them are adopted into the tribes; others are traders among them. One in particular, an elderly gentleman, called Major Twist, had left his family in New York many years before. His wife being dead, he settled among the hills, and married an Indian woman. In his youth he had, it is said, graduated at West Point and received a major's commission; but, although a gentleman of refined manners, who had been accustomed to a life of luxury, he preferred the freedom of his present associations to the rules of society, and cared for little upon his table except meat. He was aged, but not infirm nor bent with years. The sutler at Deer Creek had an Indian family, and it is said he offered to give any white man of respectability, who would marry one of his daughters, a large fortune.

While we stayed in this fort, the constant succession of visitors, anxious to see a woman and child that had escaped from Indians, kept coming in on the arrival of every train, and, with nursing my wounded husband, driving the flies from our unfortunate friend Mr. Wakefield, and attending to the wants of the child, my time was so fully occupied that I could scarcely find opportunity to entertain so many, and answer the questions they asked. Many persons seemed to think, because I had been with the savages for the space of a few hours, I understood much in regard to their characteristics.

There was a great deal of kind feeling in the garrison, and, although help was scarce, we received sympathy and good will—one kind young man, a soldier of the 11th Ohio Volunteers, named James Lindsay, offering us the loan of a hundred dollars, which favor was accepted.

Dr. Ziegler, the post surgeon, was very skilful and efficient in his care, and my husband was rapidly recovering.

The soldiers that had been sent to rescue us, having been unsuccessful in chastising the savages for the murder of their companion, were anxious to avail themselves of another opportunity, and accordingly were sent against a large party that were encamped near Platte Bridge, supposed to be hostile; but the latter proving to be friendly, or so represented by their leader, who was wounded in the affray, the soldiers returned to Deer Creek, on the 27th, and the following day we set out with them en route for Fort Laramie.

One of the instances of Indian life related to me by a mountaineer, who had travelled extensively in the western slopes of the Rocky Mountains, is as follows: Among the Shoshonees, or Snakes, is a white woman of surpassing beauty. She is held in much esteem and respect, and often consulted upon matters of importance to the tribe. She was found, when quite young, near the dead body of her brother, who had fallen in a severe conflict with a grisly bear and her two cubs. It appeared from what she remembered of the circumstances, that her father, with his family, was en route for Oregon, when they were attacked by a band of Utah Indians, and all destroyed, except herself and brother, a youth of about eighteen years of age, the attack taking place about an hour before day. While the Indians were plundering the train, her brother, taking her in his arms, sought shelter in a cave near by. This cave had long been known as a place of terror to the Utahs, and tradition had enveloped it in a cloud of mystery. It was called the "Cave of Ghosts," and the Indians carefully avoided its immediate vicinity, thus making it a place of safety for these refugees, who might have remained in its shelter until some emigrants, or a friendly band of Indians, should rescue them, had it not been for a mortal combat with three grisly bears, which resulted in her brother's death, and thus left her alone to be taken and adopted by the friendly Snakes.

The legend of the cave is known to all the Indians, and many travellers, who have visited Salt Mountain, in the Juab Valley. The cave is a remarkable depression in the earth, at the bottom of which is a clear spring of water, rising a few feet, disappearing in a porous strata, and then flowing off. The Indians call it "Pen Gun." They affirm that in this cave resides a demoniac spirit, whose form and voice is that of a child: at the sun's decline it comes up to the surface of the water, and, when any one approaches, it utters the most dismal cries for assistance, at the same time making fearful contortions of suffering. Should any

persons approach closely, their lives would surely
pay the penalty of their hardihood; it would seize
and convey them to the lower regions, to a life of
endless torture. The Utahs firmly believe in the truth
of this legend — hence its name, the Ghost Cave.

It appears that these orphans had remained undis-
covered for several months in the protecting shadow
of this retreat, when the unfortunate circumstance
took place, which deprived the brother of life and
left the little sister alone. Starting out one day upon
his hunting excursion, after bidding the little girl
take care not to ramble out of the thicket, which
screened the entrance to the cave, for fear of discovery,
he went cautiously down the cañon, and had not proceeded far, when steps behind him arrested his attention. Turning to see what it was, his eyes fell upon
a she-bear and her two cubs advancing rapidly upon
him. Hurriedly cocking his gun, he took deliberate
aim, but missed fire. In another moment she was upon
him, and tore him almost to pieces. Then the bear
left him, and when he recovered, his sister was at his
side, endeavoring to stanch his flowing blood. All
night she sat by him, and in the gray dawn of the
morning he closed his eyes in death. The weeping
child watched by the corpse of her brother, and endeavored to keep at bay the howling wolves that surrounded them, attracted by the scent of blood. She
picked up the gun and knife, and kept her solitary
watch, after loading the gun as well as she was able,
in the manner she had often observed her father and

11*

brother prepare their weapons for hunting. She only succeeded, however, in getting down a load, but was unable to cock the gun to place on a cap. As she was making the effort, a sharp war-whoop rang upon her ear, and a tall Indian stood before her, with several of his companions. The little girl, knowing the fate reserved for captives, and thinking they were the ones that murdered her parents, seized the knife and stood up resolutely in front of the dead body. The Indian, pleased at the heroic attitude of the child, reached out his hand, and smiled. For a few moments she looked at him earnestly, then burst into tears. The Indian kindly took her in his arms, and, placing her upon his pony, bore her to his people, where she still remains.

O-ko-chee was on the trail of some of the Utahs, whom he had dispersed after taking many scalps and and all their camp equipage, with many ponies. With the characteristic superstitious ideas of his people, the chieftain regarded the child as sent by the Great Spirit to his lodge. Under this belief he loaded her with favors, decorated and clothed her in costly furs, and provided captive maidens from neighboring tribes to wait upon her. She is not allowed to engage in menial employments, but is considered almost sacred. Although many have sought her hand in marriage, and rival lovers from friendly tribes have even crossed lances in combat for her love, she is still her own mistress. The daring trapper and hunter of the Rocky Mountains have braved peril and obstacles to reach her side, but in vain. The jealous chiefs of the band have carefully concealed her remarkable beauty from sight beyond the tribe, and neighboring Indians accredit her with the power of assuming invisibility. Thus this waif of the battle and the wilderness remains a mystery to all, and is only known as the Morning Star, or the White Princess of the Shoshonees.

When en route to Fort Laramie, the second afternoon, our encampment was in an extensive grove; and while some of our men were rambling about, several shots were fired at them. Supposing this an attack by savages, they returned the fire, causing quite a sensation in camp. Fortunately the timber proved a shield, and no one was injured. The invaders were travellers belonging to an emigrant train that was corralled just beyond the woods. This company was en route for the Pacific coast, and with it were some aged persons and many children.

As we travelled, the following day, we saw the body of a man who had been killed by Indians and buried by kind travellers, but now, exhumed by wolves, it lay by the roadside.

We received, through the kindness of Colonel Collins, the commander, the use of a house, and, being successful in borrowing some more money, we concluded to engage in the business of photography, and. accordingly sent to Leavenworth for the materials necessary. Savage depredations had, however, assumed such threatening proportions, that stage-travel was considered unsafe, and many obstacles lay in the way of our procuring the appliances of business as readily as we desired. Nearly two months elapsed before we received the camera, with the appurtenances, to commence business.

During our stay of five years in the far West, we have had convenient opportunity to observe border life and Indian character, the result of some of which is given in these connections; also a brief account of the experience of several women and children who became victims of Indian cruelties, which, I trust, will not be without interest to the reader.

Much has been said of the noble traits of the Indian character, but, notwithstanding, observation has confirmed our opinion that there has been a mistake somewhere. *Our* respect for "Lo the poor Indian" has been fearfully diminished, and we begin to conclude that familiarity does breed contempt, especially for the forest-king; and, if the sympathizing friends of the red man were subjected to a journey across the plains, where a visit from their savage neighbors would result in poverty and a narrow escape from death, or in a life of bondage, they would probably modify their flattering opinion; and when subsequent observation would reveal gross indolence, uncleanliness, ignorance, deception, and cruelty, they would inevitably arrive at the conclusion that, instead of the Indian being a noble lord, holding a patent of nobility from heaven, he, in truth, too often embodies the most repulsive, lazy, and unprincipled habits and attributes.

On the 8th of August, a train of twelve wagons was attacked on the emigrant road at Plum Creek, thirty miles west of Fort Kearney. A Mr. Morton, of Denver, had been to Sidney, in Clinton County, Iowa, where his wife was visiting, while he fitted himself out as a freighter for the plains. In connection with his brother-in-law and ten others, he set out upon his freighting expedition, taking with them Mrs. Morton and a little son of one of the men from Council Bluffs. When attacked, the train was completely taken by surprise, thus rendering defence useless. All the men were killed, and the woman and boy were carried away. The news of the massacre soon reached Fort Kearney, and a squad of soldiers were sent out to bury the dead, to rescue the prisoners, and also to bring the offenders to justice. This expedition failed of success, though the soldiers encamped the first night in sight of the Indians' camp. The savages had procured from the train several cases of liquors, in which they indulged freely, with the exception of two, who remained sober to guard the prisoners.

In their intoxicated condition their capture might easily have been effected, but the pursuing officer, not understanding their exposed situation, deemed it prudent to be cautious.

When the Indians set out from the place of slaughter, Mrs. Morton was placed upon a horse of vicious disposition, and not being able to control the animal, which seemed to delight in frequent plunges, she was thrown violently to the ground, much to the amuse-

I

ment of the Indians, while, for the offence of permitting herself to be thus unceremoniously dismounted, she was violently kicked by a chief.

The fall and abuse, together with grief, brought on an illness which caused her to be unable to ride that unruly animal. The chief exchanged her to two warriors for two horses. They were brothers — the two that have been mentioned as being the only sober ones in the first encampment. They took care of her, and bore her to their parents — an aged couple, living in a teepa by themselves. Their youngest daughter had died a few months before. Mrs. Morton was kindly received as an adopted child, being allowed to remain in the teepa with these old people, receiving the kindest treatment, and not being compelled to perform any hard labor. The aged chieftain seemed to pity her, and one day assured her that when he and his wife were dead she should be sent home to her own people. This was not as satisfactory, however, as she desired, and soon afterward she solicited a more favorable assurance, when he told her he would some day sell her himself for sugar and coffee. Thus relieved from toil and at rest in mind, her situation was comparatively comfortable.

These Indians, as do others, in war move about constantly, their place being here to-day, and to-morrow far distant. When Mrs. Morton was first taken with them, they had with the war-party a pretty little girl of about seven years, whom they had stolen from her home or from some emigrant train. She was an intelligent little creature, but, alas! could not understand that her only safety lay in obedience. The child cried continuously for her mother, frequently declaring she knew that the Indians intended to kill her. The savages admired the little girl, and evidently intended to take her to their village; but at length, weary of her continual fretting, a council was held to decide her fate. It was decided that she was unprofitable, and, at the close of the council, the child was placed a little apart from the others.

"I believe they are going to kill me," she cried, as she held her little, trembling hands imploringly toward her companion in bondage. "I always feared they would kill me, and I would never see my dear mamma!" At this instant a deadly arrow pierced her heart, and she lay dead.

The savages evidently were sorry for what they had done, though conceiving it their duty, and laid her to rest with all the honors due to a beloved one of their own tribe.

The little boy that had been captured with Mrs. Morton, but nine years old, felt a strong desire to escape from bondage, and confided his plans to Mrs. Morton, telling her also his intentions for future pursuit.

"If," said he, "I can escape, I will return to my mother, who, now that father is dead, needs the assistance of her oldest son; but if she casts any reproaches upon me for bondage under the Indians or for my father's death, I will leave her forever."

This child was one of the ransomed little captives who died in Denver City.

In the winter of 1864, while yet at Fort Laramie, I became aware, through acquaintance with some friendly Indians, of the presence of a white woman in a village fifty miles north of Platte Bridge, and communicated the fact to the commandant, who made other inquiries, and finally offered a ransom for her, when a Mr. Reshaw, an old and wealthy mountaineer, sent his son, a half-breed Indian, to pay their price, and bring the woman to his house. This fellow, unfortunately, rendering himself obnoxious to the lady, she communicated the fact to the aged chieftain, and begged to be allowed another escort.

The old man was astonished and angry, and immediately commanded that the "white man's son" be brought before him; then, with a contemptuous expression, the old man ordered him to take his presents of sugar, coffee, blankets, horses, etc., and to leave the village, "For," said he, "I will not let the white woman go with you. A man of honor shall come for her, or I will wait until the snows have left the ground, and then carry her to the fort myself." This decision was final, and the mountaineer's son was obliged to return without accomplishing his mission. A few weeks after, another son of a mountaineer went, and, after paying seventeen hundred dollars, bore her away to Fort Laramie, where she was hospitably entertained in the family of Mr. Bullock. On the way from Fort Casper to Laramie, Mrs. Mor-

RETURNING TO CIVILIZATION.

ton saw, at Fort Deer-Creek, an Indian called Black
Crow, who had been one of the band that had murdered her husband and the other men belonging to
that train, also abducting her.   This fact she communicated to the Provost Marshal, Lieutenant Triggs,
who immediately sent for the offender.   He was taken
at Fort Deer-Creek, where he had established himself and his family for a winter's support, and brought
to Fort Laramie, where he was tried, condemned, and
executed with the two other Indians before mentioned
— Two-Face and Black Bear.   The 9th of August,
1864, Black Bear and Two-Face, with a party of
their men, made a raid upon a settlement on Blue
River, east of Fort Kearney, killing several men, and
abducting two women and some children.

A Mrs. Ewbanks and Miss Roper were the unfortunate ladies that were carried away.   They were returning from a neighbor's house, and discovered the
Indians in time to conceal themselves among the tall
grass, where they might have escaped discovery if it
had not been for the sobs of Mrs. Ewbanks and the
cries of her infant.

They were taken to an Indian village, about a hundred miles southeast of Denver City, and there they
met Mrs. Morton — being permitted to remain together for six weeks; but fear of the wrath of the
savages, together with the uncertainty of finding a
settlement, discouraged them from any attempt to
escape.   In the following autumn, Miss Roper and
three children were ransomed at a fort south of Den-

12

ver City by the military authorities. The four captives being expected at the fort, the commandant went out to meet them, when a dear little girl of two years, who was tied upon the back of a squaw, as if conscious of her near release, and anxious to be restored to the loving care of her own people, stretched out her little hands imploringly, which sight touched the hearts of all who witnessed the scene, recalling to them tender memories of loved ones at home, while tears rose unbidden to many eyes.

Mrs. Ewbanks, her infant, and Mrs. Morton were soon afterward carried beyond the Platte River, and separated. Mrs. Ewbanks, with her child, remained with the Indians until April, 1865, when, by a stratagem of the commandant, she was brought to Fort Laramie by Two-Face and Black Bear. These Indians, thinking to increase their fortunes, purchased Mrs. Ewbanks and her child of another chief, who held her for a slave. They soon afterward set out en route for Fort Laramie, and, when they arrived within a few miles of the fort, the prisoners were left with a small company, while Two-Face preceded them to arrange the terms of sale. The commander readily agreed to the price they asked, which was one thousand dollars, and, on the subsequent day, Mrs. Ewbanks and her babe were brought in.

They crossed the Platte River five miles below the fort, near Beauvais' ranch, and in the passage of this stream the prisoners suffered intensely. The child was bound upon the mother's back, and she secured to a log, to which the end of a long rope was fastened; the other end of the rope was attached to the chieftain's saddle, and he, passing over, pulled the log of wood along with the prisoners. The chief passed over readily, without discomfort; but the mother and child were almost frozen when they reached the opposite bank, as the water was very cold, being covered with floating ice, and the sufferers only having one garment in this inclement season.

At the ranch they were dressed, and soon the chieftains proceeded with them to the fort, conducting them to the commander, who, instead of paying the price that had been promised, seized the chiefs, and caused them to be confined in the guard-house to await a trial. Being found guilty of murder, they were condemned and executed, as above stated, together with Black Crow.

Before the execution, Black Bear sent a few dollars in money to Mrs. Ewbanks, with the message that he had no further use for it, and it might be made useful to her and her child.

Mrs. Ewbanks remained at Fort Laramie for several weeks, until a company of soldiers, commanded by Captain Fouts, of the Iowa Volunteers, went down the country. Here Mrs. Ewbanks narrowly escaped death by the Indians. A band of friendly red men, who had been living near Fort Laramie, were being taken to Fort Kearney, it being regarded as a more suitable place for them. At noon, on the first day's march, the Indians became suspicious that some treachery was intended, and that they were being decoyed to their destruction. This mistake may have arisen from some indiscretion on the part of some of the soldiers, who amused themselves by throwing the papooses into the river, and watching their dexterity in swimming out. Nothing was said by the swarthy fathers and brothers, but their looks toward each other showed plainly that their minds were not on thoughts of peace. Toward evening, they affected a desire to hunt, and begged the captain for some powder, which he generously and unsuspectingly gave them. This alarmed some of the soldiers, who requested that a supply of ammunition be given them, but were refused. Soon after, the Indians went out to shoot birds, and on their return said that one of their young men had been bitten by a snake. An old squaw came to Mrs. Ewbanks, begging that she would go with her to the sick man, and endeavor to relieve his sufferings. Mrs. Ewbanks, not suspecting any treachery, immediately arose to accompany her, but being cautioned by Mrs. Fouts and others, desisted, and, as the Indian recovered, no more notice was taken of the circumstance.

When they were ready to resume the journey, the Indians, with one simultaneous shout, fell upon the soldiers, who, being without ammunition, were unable successfully to resist, and several were killed. The savages, having succeeded in spreading consternation and death, fled beyond the Platte River. One Indian, however, was chained in a wagon, having been de-tained a prisoner at Fort Laramie. This Indian fell a victim to the wrath of the soldiers, who took him from the wagon and shot him. On perceiving intimations that they would destroy him, he turned a look of defiance and a scornful smile upon his white captors. When he lay dead, a mountaineer, who had witnessed the whole proceedings, and who was a friend to the Indians, sprang upon the lifeless form, and with one stroke of a knife severed the scalp, offering it to a soldier. Next he cut off an arm, and so continued to mutilate the body till the pieces were all distributed among the lookers-on, all the while giving way to vituperation against the soldiers. Captain Fouts, the officer who commanded the execution, had been one of the first to fall. A reason given by some for this unexpected outbreak was a feeling of ill-will for this officer. Captain Fouts had been a Methodist clergyman for twenty-five years before entering the army. He left a wife and several children, who witnessed his untimely fate.

In the summer of 1864, which witnessed so many bloody scenes in the West, there lived on the emigrant road, fifty miles east of Denver City, a Mr. Morrison and his family, who were startled by the sudden appearance of Indians at their door. When all hope of saving the women and children was gone, Mr. Morrison endeavored to save himself by swimming the Platte River, but was shot while in the water, and his lifeless body floated down with the current. His little boy, an adopted child, was never

12 *

heard of again. Possibly he now roams the hills amid the surroundings of savage life.

Mrs. Morrison and her infant, a child of one year, were carried away. The child died from injuries received from the stamping feet of a chief, who became angry at the disinclination of the little one to play with him when he insisted on being amused; but the mother was ransomed after a year's servitude with the Sioux.

Many white women were seen among these Indians. The following narrative reveals the history of one who was the wife of Black Bear, and possibly the Indian of that name that was executed at Fort Laramie.

In the year 1852, an emigrant train en route for California had arrived in the neighborhood of the crossing of the North Platte, and, the cholera breaking out among the travellers, one after another was seized with this epidemic, until all, except one little girl, died. Black Bear, in hunting, came to the wagons—now transformed into a lazaretto—and received a letter from the hand of the dying father, with prayerful injunctions to carry the dear little creature to his home in the East, where he would be rewarded by the child's friends, in addition to the heavy purse he then gave him. Black Bear took the little girl, and the money, and everything left of the train, to his home among the hills, and, as his views did not coincide with the directions of the dying father, allowed the girl to run about like a little savage, which she soon became, forgetting her name, language, and

MEETING A WHITE WOMAN IN THE INDIAN CAMP.

family, but knew she was white. This knowledge she attributed to have discovered in the brook, as she sat with her red companions and their images were reflected; but her protector still retained the letter which explained the facts. Arriving at a marriageable age, Black Bear took her for his wife, and when seen in the village she had one child, a little Indian boy, and was, except in blonde complexion, an Indian squaw, submitting to her lot and its savage surroundings.

A little boy of fourteen years, whose name proved to be Charles Sylvester, from Quincy, Illinois, had been stolen, when but seven years old, from his parents, who were at that time in Humboldt Valley, Utah Territory. The knowledge that he was not an Indian, but a white child, never left him, though he had forgotten his people, language, and even his own name. He had become so domesticated in the habits of the Indians that no fears of losing him ever seemed to occur to them, and he was allowed full liberty. He had been with these Indians seven years, when he escaped and came to a military station, where he had some difficulty in convincing the officer that he was not an Indian boy. Eventually, however, he succeeded in making his story intelligible, and was sent to St. Louis, where he was advertised, and, it is said, his portrait was widely circulated. A gentleman from Quincy, Illinois, furnished satisfactory proof that the boy was his nephew, and was allowed to take him home. Little Charles proved to be very bright, and in a few months had acquired quite a knowledge of the English language, learning also to read. His love for his own people, however, was not strong enough to draw his affections from the habits of his life, and the restraints of his city home were irksome to him. Having a hasty temper, he became offended at some remark made by his uncle, and immediately started to join the Indians, among whom he still remains, acting as a trader and interpreter, at North Platte City, Nebraska, on the Union Pacific Railroad. There the noted chief, Spotted Tail, held his band, and, though considered peaceful, was in communication with the hostile tribes.

Near Spotted Tail's rendezvous two little boys were riding together on one horse, when they were pierced by an arrow which entered both, pinning them together as they sat in the saddle. In this condition the little fellows rode home, where the weapon was extracted, and, strange to say, they recovered. Near the same place, three ladies were captured and carried off: two of them were young girls, named Kennedy; the other a Norwegian. Three months after their abduction they were ransomed and brought to North Platte City.

CHAPTER XI.

IN the spring of 1848, a pleasant party, with highly-
wrought visions of the then newly-discovered gold-
fields of California, left East Medway, Massachusetts,
for an overland journey across the plains. Among the
party was James P. Kimball, then only nineteen years
of age, and just married to Jane McNiel, half-sister of
the famous Kit Carson. The father and mother of the
bride accompanied them. Everything prospered, and
all went merry as a marriage-bell, the company having
been increased to sixty-three in number, when they
set out on their overland journey. They reached the
foot of Chilicothe Mountain, June 15, 1848, having
crossed the plains of Utah. There they were suddenly
attacked by a war-party of the Snakes and Shoshonees,
and the entire company captured or killed. Kimball
was successful in saving his own life, and that of his
wife, by more than once successfully running the
gauntlet for both. The Indians, forming themselves

141

into two lines, gave him the chance of running between them, promising that, if he succeeded in gaining
the other end of the line, escaping kicks, the deadly
thrust of knives, and the blows of tomahawks, twice —
once for himself, once for his wife — they would spare
him, and take him into their favor, together with his
wife, adopting them into the tribe.

His father and mother-in-law, however, fell victims to their fiendish customs, and were burned at the
stake. When the Indians had satisfied their cruel
barbarity, they took their captives, and hurried away
to the Columbia River, in Washington Territory, the
headquarters of the tribe, where young Kimball was
soon exalted into a distinguished personage, becoming
the second chief in the tribe. After several months,
they made preparations for another expedition, and
Kimball and his wife accompanied them. Starting
down the Columbia, they encountered the Enagos,
suffering great loss and signal defeat. Among many
captured was the wife of Kimball, who was carried
away, and remained a prisoner and slave for two
years and a half, when another war terminated in
the defeat of the Enagos and the restoration of Mrs.
Kimball to her husband. The Snakes and Shoshonees
acted as one tribe, although with different head men
or chiefs.

For the remaining fifteen years of their captivity,
the Kimballs followed the fortunes of the tribe, wandering here and there over a vast region of country —
at some seasons well supplied with game, at other

times, often compelled to subsist upon insects, roots, and herbs.

One very hot day a dark cloud suddenly seemed to pass before the sun and threaten a great storm. The wind rose and the cloud became still darker, until the light of the sun was almost hidden. A few drops sprinkled the earth like falling snow-flakes, and then, in a heavy, blinding, and apparently inexhaustible shower, fell a countless swarm of grasshoppers, covering the ground and almost darkening the air in their descent. It is almost impossible to convey an idea of their extent. They seemed to rival Pharaoh's locusts in number, and would, no doubt, have done damage to the vegetation of the savages, had not the insects themselves fallen victims to the keen appetites of the red men. At such times there is a general jubilee in collecting these insects. For this purpose various methods are resorted to: a very common one is to dig large holes in the ground; these are filled with weeds, grass, and other combustible material, which is lighted; into these apertures the grasshoppers are driven by energetic juveniles; then the fires are removed, when the heat of the ground bakes them. All join in at such an event with the greatest avidity, and what is considered a scourge in civilization, is to the Indian a blessing. The savages save as many as possible in the time of their stay, and as that is very uncertain, it is consequently a busy time.

During the entire period, the Kimballs kept an accurate account of the years, by means of the passing of the seasons.   The reputation of Mr. Kimball waxed greater, until he became a medical man of the tribe. Finally, in one of their excursions toward the frontier, they joined in an attack near ,a fort, and, during the progress of the fight, Mr. Kimball gave some soldiers to understand that he was a white man, desiring to escape from bondage.   He was soon recaptured by Lieutenant Wyman, of the 18th United States Infantry.   Before leaving the Indians, Mr. Kimball went to his wife's tent, informed her of his prospects, and hastened with her to the pickets, where they were kindly welcomed.   They received attention from Colonel Carrington, commanding at Fort Kearny, Nebraska, who helped them on their way to their old home in the East.   They left behind two daughters, who were married to chiefs — Peter Folsome and John Hawkeye, who are now in the Sweetwater gold regions.

After arriving at Elmira, New York, Mr. Kimball was fortunate in ascertaining that his father still lived, but that he had changed his place of residence, and settled upon a farm near Paine's Post, engaged in farming and mercantile business.   The appearance of the son and his wife must have been like those having risen from the grave, as seventeen years before they had been supposed to be murdered upon the plains. At the time of the recapture, Mr. Kimball received a ball through his left wrist, and also an arrow wound.

Elizabeth Blackwell, a young lady of more than

ordinary beauty, migrated with her parents to the regions of Salt Lake City, where they united with the Church of the Latter-day Saints, and, like many others, had not resided there long, ere a vision was received by the head of the family, directing him to take another wife—one, by the way, that was more comely than Mrs. Blackwell, Elizabeth's mother.

This practical version of the doctrine of the church produced a little unpleasantness in the family, and, although it was inculcated in the doctrine that submission was a duty in a wife and children, Elizabeth and her mother could not understand the moral, and ventured, indiscreetly, it seems, to remonstrate against this innovation in family matters. The husband and father, however, in accordance with the custom of that people, brought home his second wife, and she, very naturally, supplanted the faithful old wife of his youth and the mother of his children, who found herself neglected, and even abused. Finally, matters reached a crisis. This injustice could no longer be endured without rebellion, and, acting upon that conclusion, the family was not a happy one. Mr. Blackwell, in one of his attempts to produce good order in the house, and govern the family according to principles inculcated by the believers of the Mormon Church, proceeded to inflict summary punishment upon Mrs. Blackwell, senior. Though Elizabeth was a member of the church, she had not been convinced that this was one of the duties of a husband, and, therefore, ventured to remonstrate, taking

13   K

her mother's part with an earnestness that caused her father to vent his indignation upon her. He vainly attempted her subjugation, and in one of his flourishes with a knife he destroyed one of poor Elizabeth's eyes.

Unable to endure longer the abuse and oppression of the tyrannical and inhuman father, the wretched mother, with her three children, attempted to escape from this land of promise, and, though danger surrounded them on every hand, they started toward an emigrant road, which they had ascertained lay to the east, near Fort Bridger. Having had little experience in a mountainous country, and being overtaken by a violent snow-storm, they became bewildered, and lost their way. Night set in, with cold and tempestuous weather, and, during the night, the mother and one of her daughters died, and in the morning another died. It appeared that they were unable to procure a fire, on account of the absence of matches, and thus were unprotected from the inclemency of the weather, save by the inadequate clothing upon their persons. All day and all night they had wandered through the freezing cold, until, overcome with fatigue, they took shelter in a cañon — the drifting snow, like a white shroud, shutting out the world forever from the eyes of the feeble mother and two of her children. When the rising sun appeared, it kissed the pale cheek of the dead and dying, and the solitary flight of a vulture, as he encircled the anticipated feast with croaks of triumph, was all that could be seen, save the unbroken surface of the sparkling snow.

Some Indians, attracted by the ominous flight of the circling bird, sought the spot, ariving just in time to save Elizabeth from death, but, alas! not from mutilation.

Taking her up, they bore her to their camp, where, with unremitting care, her life was saved, but her limbs were so badly frozen that amputation of both became necessary, and they were taken off above the knee.

The kindness she received from these Indians so won her affection, that she prefers to remain with them ; and they, with the superstitious notions so common among Indians, regard her as one sent to them by the Great Spirit.

She is able to relate many instances of Indian life, one or two of which are quite interesting. We give them briefly: One day, a young woman was brought into camp, and as a warrior stepped to the side of the horse to assist in dismounting, she drew a pistol and shot him through the heart. She was immediately condemned to suffer death by torture, and was, accordingly, tied to a stake, when very many small gashes were cut in her body and limbs, these filled with gunpowder, and finally ignited with hot irons. The wretched woman's screams were dreadful, and, being mingled with the jeers of her tormentors, were more than Elizabeth Blackwell could endure to hear. She begged that the suffering woman might be relieved by death, if they would not let her live; which request was granted, and a tomahawk ended her misery.

These Indians sometimes capture little children and bring them up as their own. The history of one of these is given in the following narrative: A squaw had seen a little girl of about twelve years playing near her father's house, and determined to secure her. For this purpose she placed herself in ambush near the child, who was gathering wild flowers, and, springing upon her, covered her head with a buffalo-robe. She carried the child to the Indian camp, which was in the neighborhood. The father of this squaw had, a few weeks before, lost by death a daughter of about the same age as the stolen child, and, upon receiving the little prisoner, adopted her as his own, and sent a party to destroy her father's house with all its inmates. The little girl was named "Bluebird," because of the color of her eyes.

For three years she was guarded with jealous care, and every effort was made to cause her to forget her own people. At the expiration of that time she was given to the chief's son in marriage; but, very naturally, the poor girl could not love the untutored savage thus forced upon her, and her dislike, so evident and unequivocal, produced a feeling of resentment in the bosom of the young chief, which vented itself in abuse on his unwilling wife. One year after their marriage a daughter was born; but the mother never recovered, and in three months died; leaving her helpless child to lead a life of savage wanderings.

Elizabeth Blackwell's father soon became tired of his Mormon wife and the restraints of the saints; so, taking to the mountains, he became a noted highwayman, and after some years, hearing of his daughter's residence among the Indians, he visited her, and gave her a large amount of his stolen money. Returning to civilization, and continuing in his downward career, he was taken by the Vigilance Committee, at Virginia City, Montana, and executed.

In the summer of 1865, a Mr. Fletcher and his family were travelling with a train en route for Oregon. He had one beautiful daughter, who fell in love with a young physician. They walked, rode, and sang together, after the manner of young people. But this did not coincide with Mr. Fletcher's views of propriety, and he detached his teams from the large train, thus travelling by themselves, leaving the young man behind, and breaking off the intercourse of the lovers. The second day of their journey alone, Mr. Fletcher and his family were attacked by a party of five hundred Indians. The large train protected itself, but these, unfortunately, with all their effects, fell into the hands of the Indians.

Mrs. Fletcher was horribly mutilated, being cut into small pieces. Her husband was wounded, and, endeavoring to escape to the train, was shot again by a savage that pursued him and took his horse, leaving the body upon the ground where it had fallen. A

13*

little boy was instantly killed, but a little girl of five years was taken on the journey for the space of two days, when, becoming tired of the care of her, they dashed her head to pieces against a rock. Miss Fletcher was carried away and retained a prisoner for one year, when she was exchanged for merchandise. On her return home she expressed no particular desire to go to her people; but, on the contrary, seemed entirely resigned to her fate with the Indians, saying she had been to blame, and deserved to be punished.

The Indian village near Fort Laramie was a place of amusement for every person belonging to the garrison. Even women and children sometimes visited it to hear the squaws and papooses talk. Though the language is a mere jargon, when mixed with English and accompanied by signs it is not difficult to understand.

The Indians that were perpetrating these outrages were the same that escaped justice two years before, after committing an indiscriminate slaughter in Minnesota. One of these friendly Indians told of being in the Minnesota war, and being taken sick — not, however, until he had killed several persons — and, compelled by illness to linger behind, was overtaken by a squad of soldiers, who carried him to their fort, took him in, and tenderly cared for him. When he recovered from his illness they supplied him with clothing, gave him meat for his journey, and sent him to his mother, cautioning him, however, to fight no more. Here he laughed derisively at the idea of an

Indian brave abandoning his profession. He told of several instances of the outrageous cruelties of his band in their marauding and murderous attacks in Minnesota, one of which is particularly shocking. An infant was taken from its mother's arms and placed in a bake-oven that was heated before the fire, then the scorching lid was placed over it. The sight so agonized the mother, that, disregarding herself, she struggled frantically to force her way to her child, but was stabbed through and through, falling dead even before her baby's sufferings were ended.

Several little girls they captured and carried away, but they survived the savage treatment, and were ransomed at Fort Pierre.

A dear cousin of my own was murdered some years ago in Nevada. I believe, however, that the circumstance has not been narrated for the public, and I relate it in connection with the foregoing accounts.

Mr. Jones, with his wife and children, were emigrating to Oregon, and when they had arrived in the Humboldt Valley, he was taken with sudden sickness, and they were compelled to stop for a while. Finding a hunter's deserted cabin near the road, they took possession of it. The Indians were reported hostile, having committed several outrages upon emigrants, though to no great extent.

Mr. Jones grew worse, and his death was every hour expected, and though he pleaded that Mrs. Jones should save herself and the children, she resolutely refused to leave her husband in this critical hour, trusting in God's mercy for safety.

The second night of their stay in the cabin, after seeing the two youngest children peacefully sleeping, she took her seat with the eldest, a bright boy of eight years, by her husband's bedside. Suddenly a noise, resembling the cry of the whippoorwill, attracted their attention, and a fearful foreboding of danger pervaded their minds. Mrs. Jones stepped to the door and looked out into the darkness, but could see nothing, nor was the noise of the whippoorwill to be heard; and returning to her husband, she had scarcely seated herself, when footsteps without startled her. She made a movement for her husband's gun, when the frail door fell into pieces upon the floor, and a number of fierce savages, immediately rushing into the room, instantly shot Mr. Jones through the head. She sprang forward as she saw her husband's blood gush from the wound, and, with the courage of despair, shot the murderer. Immediately their weapons were turned upon her, and she fell, mortally wounded, by her dead husband's side.

The little boy, having witnessed the death of his father, and beheld his mother fall, and realizing his lonely situation, with noble fortitude presented himself to the chief, and, baring his youthful breast, begged to share the fate of his parents. The savage raised his gun, but it missed fire, and the child stood unhurt. Again the gun snapped, with the same result; when the chief, influenced by a superstitious feeling, which

DEATH OF MRS. JONES.

prevails among all Indians, and astonished with the
remarkable daring of the child, forbore; and placing
the weapon of death upon the floor, he commanded
the boy to save himself and the other children.   The
little boy immediately sought his dying mother's side,
and telling her the chief's order, inquired what she
would have him do with the children.   The mother,
realizing that her counsel was all she could give her
little ones in that moment of peril, kissed and blessed
them, telling him to take the children, and find a path
that led across the country, one or two miles, to the place
where she had been told a hunter lived.   The boy, con-
trolling his emotions, and inspired with precocious wisdom to aid him in his arduous duties and responsibili-
ties, listened while his dying parent told him what she
desired him to do for himself and the helpless little ones
she was leaving forever.   She commended the younger
ones to his brotherly care, with an injunction to obedience on their part, and, when her glazing eyes were setting in death, saw them depart into the darkness on their
perilous and uncertain journey, while her soul fluttered on the threshold of eternity, praying for their
welfare to the God in whose presence she would soon
appear.   She was immediately taken from the house,
and fires lighted, and thus ended her life.

When the children arrived at the place of their
expected refuge, they found, to their dismay, that
the hut was deserted, for the occupants had been
slaughtered by the savages.   What to do was a serious question for the little brother to decide, as he con-

tinued wandering about the pathless wilderness,
wearily to watch for the skulking savages that might
beset their way, and to gain what little nourishment
they might from leaves and bark, hoping that God,
in his mercy, would guide them to some friendly
cabin, or remove them to himself.   In this lonely condition they spent that day and the next, but on the
third, to their awakening horror, they saw a savage
approaching.

Terrible experience had made the eldest boy a hero,
and knowing no phase of Indian character but fiendish brutality, he gathered a pile of stones, and station-
ing himself in front of his brother and baby sister,
with his father's pocket-knife in his hand, resolved to
defend himself and them to the last.

The Indian drew near, surprised to see the children
there, and, when he beheld the boy's preparation for
defence, he laughed, and in signs assured him of his
friendly disposition, which the boy at first disbelieved,
but finally the Indian succeeded in convincing them
that he intended no harm.

It is pleasant to find any palliation of savage
cruelty, and this Indian proved himself to be a rare
exception to the ferocious rule.   He took the little
orphans in a canoe down a river, and stopping at intervals, went ashore to gather bark, berries, and roots
to feed them, showing a truly kind and amiable disposition in all his actions.

The younger children suffered terribly from the exposure and meagre fare, and when, after a journey of two

hundred miles, they arrived at a settlement of civilized people, were so reduced as to be unable to stand on their feet.

Some emigrants kindly carried the little orphans to San Francisco, where a benefit was given them in a theatre, and their story was made into ballad form and sung with great effect by a young vocalist, named Miss Fanny Blodgett. Their uncle, John Smail, who was then residing in Oregon, being informed of the sad fate of his sister and her husband, with the helpless condition of the children, immediately came for them, and carried them East to their relatives, placing them under excellent care, and, as far as possible, supplying the place of their parents. The two younger children have since died, but the eldest lives, and bids fair to fulfil his early and precocious promise.

Four women, that were stolen by savages from Minnesota in 1862, were brought into the country northwest of Fort Laramie. One was a young girl, who gave her name as Mary Boshea, and said she was the daughter of a Frenchman, who lived near Spirit Lake, Minnesota. The family were all murdered, except Mary, whose life was spared for years of slavery with the hostile Sioux. One year she was treated as a child, then taken for the wife of a warrior, and possibly to-day roams the hills with her savage companions. One of the others, being unable to travel, was shot, while crossing a creek on a beaver dam, fell off, and sank in the water. The others were one Mrs. Wright and Mrs. Dooley.

The former had one child, a little boy, whom the Indians killed, and left unburied by the side of a path that was frequented for wood and water, and the afflicted mother was compelled to go frequently by the spot where the decaying body of her child lay, but she dared not turn aside to place a covering upon the little body.

I have been told that Mrs. Wright was finally ransomed at Fort Pierre, and, that immediately on arriving at Yankton, a small town on the Missouri River, she applied to the Legislature, that happened to be in session at that time, for a bill of divorcement from her husband, urging, as her reason, his cruelty in leaving her and their child in jeopardy when the Indians came upon them.

The husband, learning of his wife's presence in town, hastened to meet her, and she, not knowing that he was in that section of the country, answered the call of the door-bell, and saw her husband. Their eyes met. She gave one scream, and fled from his sight to her own room.

At this unkind reception from one he had so long mourned as dead, or lost forever, the sorrowful husband sat down and wept.

The kind-hearted landlady, compassionating his sorrow, undertook to plead his cause with the heart-broken wife, and at last succeeded in gaining her consent to an interview, when a reconciliation was effected. At the time of Mrs. Wright's ransom she had pleaded vainly for the ransom of poor Mary Boshea.

Mrs. Dooley's children, five in number, were all murdered. Her husband had been wounded and left for dead, but finally recovered. Mrs. Dooley's grief was greater than her reason could bear. When in her own happy home, she was a lady of more than ordinary intelligence and beauty, but when she was ransomed at Fort Pierre it was too late, and she was carried to an insane asylum, whither her broken-hearted husband soon afterward followed her.

An extremely interesting account of the Hermit of the Gila is related by a returned captive from the Apaches, who inhabit the country north of the wild and picturesque river which is a part of the boundary line between the Republic of Mexico and the United States. This region abounds in scenery of the most sublime description. Cañons of hundreds of miles in extent, through which rush mighty rivers, and mountains of the most bold and stupendous outline, mock the attempt to convey, by description, their sublime order and beauty. Not only is it magnificent in outline, but it is also curious in detail. Hundreds of miles in extent are covered with huge pyramidal rocks, which appear like the remains of ancient fortifications, where battlements and towers rise one after another in indescribable grandeur. Again, the ruins of Egyptian greatness and skill seem to be represented by these fantastic grottos, gloomily frowning above the plains, over which the wild Apache drives his herds, or lazily saunters in quest of game. Nor are these wild mockeries of man's skill and aspirations alone

14

the attractions, for mingled with them are the ruins of cities and nations that have passed away. The rude tombs of kings and princes lie here, half buried in the accumulated dust of centuries, mocking the futile effort of the antiquarian to fathom the mystery of their origin. It is only conjecture that ascribes these ruins to the Aztecs, the warlike nation that built the beautiful city of Mexico, and perished in the ashes of their own dwellings. Amid these decaying ruins are found fragments of their cooking-utensils, mirrors of Iztli, and fragments of sculpture-work representing their deity, "Huitzilopochtli." These silent monuments of the forgotten past lay scattered over a vast country, abandoned to the lizard and the tarantula, who crawl over these unknown relics of the past to stretch themselves unmolested under the rays of the morning sun. Around on every hand curiosities of nature abound, making it look like the work of enchantment. These objects of sublime interest differ greatly in their formation, as well as in their external appearance; some consisting of hard clay, others of rock almost as white as the drifting snow, gypsum bluffs, and huge sandstone boulders and cliffs; some again having a dark hue, being, in reality, anthracite and bituminous coal formations — high columns rising from the earth like the mammoth trees of California, from twenty to thirty feet in diameter, as round and true in their outlines as if they had been moulded by the hand of art. These columns are surrounded by huge rings, projecting many feet around, and making their summits inaccessible to almost all living things,

except the birds of the air.   Upon entering still farther among them, these columns and shafts blend into
one common mass, and present the appearance of a
grand roof supported by innumerable pillars, while
the outward surroundings are covered with sand
dotted with cactus and small trees.   In these dark
recesses the huge grisly bear and mountain lion find
a safe retreat from the hunter, while the overhanging
rocks form desirable positions for clusters of bats and
owls.   Howling wolves make the deep recesses echo
with their lonely cry of hunger and defiance.   Upon
the summits of the loftiest peaks the American eagle
surveys the plains below, or scours the valleys to
find food for the young eaglets in their eyry.   And
over all the California vulture sweeps, secure alike
from man and beast, and in majesty defiantly pursues
his lonely flight.

The effect of artificial light upon these wonders of
nature is indeed grand.   A torch in the darkness of
night almost endows these grotesque forms with life
and animation, calling to mind Milton's description
of the infernal regions, where the council of the leading spirits of evil held their deliberations, and planned
a war against Heaven.   Among these rocks lived a
hermit, who was not a native of the country, and none
knew whence he came, or how long he had been there.
Much of his life had been spent among these hills,
sleeping at night in crevices and caverns which the hand
of nature had formed.   His food consisted of wild fruits
and herbs, together with such game as he could trap
and snare.   His only drink was water from a brook,

from which he also drew some small fish with hooks made from bone. His clothing consisted of such skins as he was able to obtain, and they were sewed together with sinews. He wore the hair-side out, and with a belt secured it around his waist.

The Indians believed him to be some supernatural being, and carefully avoided him; they supposing him to be the remnant of some inoffensive people, that had been lost in an earthquake, and connected him with the remarkable ruins which surrounded his abode. This mystery which enveloped him was the secret of his security, for other intruders coming to the country were swept without mercy from the earth by the fierce and warlike chiefs.

I was mournfully struck with the desolate expression of this man's countenance. He was evidently on the verge of eternity, and, looking back over a long life, he could not but acknowledge it a misspent one, since not one talent had he rendered back to his Great Master. His head was covered with long gray hair, which fell upon his shoulders, and his white beard fell upon his breast. One thin hand grasped a rude cane, while the other clasped a door-post of his hut to support his bowed and trembling form.

I listened while he told his story as to his motive in coming there; how fifty years of his life had been wasted; why he had become disgusted with the world, and had withdrawn from it. In a rock he said he had dug a sepulchre for his body; but who, thought I, as I received his blessing and bade him adieu, will roll a stone to the door?

CHAPTER XII.

THE main object sought to be secured by the treaty
of Laramie, of July, A. D. 1866, was the opening
of a new route to Montana from Fort Laramie, via
Bridger's Ferry and the head-waters of the Powder,
Tongue, and Big Horn rivers.

This country was occupied by the Ogallalla and
Minnecòngoux band of Sioux, the Northern Cheyenne and Arappahoe tribes, and the Mountain Crows.
The region through which the road was to pass, and
does pass, is the most attractive and valuable to the
Indians. It abounds with game. Flocks of mountain
sheep, droves of elk and deer, and herds of buffalo
range through and live in this country, and the
Indians with propriety call it their " last, best hunting-
grounds." All these Indians were reluctant to allow
the proposed road to pass through these hunting-
grounds; but all would reluctantly assent to this for
so liberal an equivalent as the Government was willing to give. The Indians were required further to
stipulate that the Government should have the right
to establish one or more military posts on this road,
in their country. All the Indians occupying it refused

thus to stipulate, and the chiefs, head men, and warriors protested against the establishment of any military post on their hunting-grounds, along that road, north of Fort Reno.

While negotiations were going on with Red Cloud and their leading chiefs, to induce them to yield to the Government the right peacefully to establish these military posts, (which right they persistently refused to yield, saying it was asking too much of their people —asking all they had—for it would drive away all their *game*,) Colonel H. B. Carrington, 18th United States Infantry, with about seven hundred officers and men, arrived at Laramie, en route to their country, to establish and occupy military posts along the Montana road, pursuant to General Orders No. 33, from the headquarters of the Department of the Missouri, March 10, 1866, Major General Pope commanding. The destination and purpose of Colonel Carrington and his command were communicated to their chiefs. They seemed to construe this into a determination on the part of the Government to occupy their country by military posts, even without their consent, or that of their people, and, as soon as practicable, they withdrew from the council, with their adherents, refusing to accept any presents from the commissioners, returned to their country, and, with a strong force of warriors, commenced a vigorous and relentless war against all whites who came into it, including citizens and soldiers. Quite a large number of Indians, who did not occupy the country along the road, were anxious to make a treaty and

remain at peace. Some of this class had resided near
Fort Laramie, others (Brules) occupied the White-
earth River valley and the Sand Hills south of that
river. The commmissioners appointed several of the
leading warriors of these Indians as chiefs, viz.: Big
Mouth, Spotted Tail, Swift Bear, and Two-Strike.
A portion of these Indians have remained near Fort
Laramie, and a portion of them on the Republican
Fork of the Kansas River, and have strictly complied
with their treaty stipulations.

The number of Sioux Indians who considered
themselves bound by the treaty, and who have remained at peace, is about two thousand, while the
Ogallalla and Brule bands, the Northern Cheyennes
and Arrapahoes, with a few Sans Arcs, numbering in
the aggregate about six hundred, remained in their
old country, and went to war under their old chiefs,
and, by conquest, after bloody wars, saved their country from invasion and occupation by the whites. This
war has been carried on by the Indians with most
extraordinary vigor and unwonted success. From
July 26th, the day on which Lieutenant Wand's train
was attacked, to the 21st day of December, on which
Brevet Lieutenant-Colonel Fetterman, with his command of eighty officers and men, was overpowered and
massacred, they killed ninety-one enlisted men and
five officers of our army, and fifty-eight citizens, and
wounded twenty more, capturing and driving away
three hundred and six oxen and cows, three hundred
and four mules, and one hundred and sixty-one horses.

During this time they appeared in front of Fort Philip Kearney, making hostile demonstrations and committing hostile acts fifty-one different times, and attacked nearly every train and person that attemped to pass over the Montana road.

The following account of the massacre of Lieutenant-Colonel Fetterman's party includes the causes which led to it:

General Order, No. 33, from the headquarters of the Department of the Missouri, dated March 10, 1866, directed that two new military posts should be established on the new route to Montana — one " near the base of the Big Horn Mountains," the other " on or near the Upper Yellowstone," and designated the 2d battalion of the 18th Infantry to garrison the three posts on this route, created the Mountain District, Department of the Platte, and directed the colonel of the regiment (Colonel H. B. Carrington) to take his post at Fort Reno, and command the district, which included all the troops and garrisons on that route.

General Order, No. 7, from the headquarters of the Department of the Platte, June 23, 1866, directed that the 2d battalion of the 18th Infantry should take posts as follows: Two companies at Fort Reno, on Powder River; two companies about eighty miles nearly south of Fort Reno, on the waters of the Powder or Tongue River, which post should be known as Fort Philip Kearney; and two companies at the crossing of the Big Horn River, on the same road, and about seventy miles beyond Fort Philip Kearney, to be known as Fort C. F. Smith, directing that the colonel of the regiment should take post at Fort Philip Kearney, to command the "Mountain District."

The orders above referred to were issued with the express understanding, apparently, that this road to Montana was to be opened through the Indian country by compact or treaty with the savages occupying it, and not by conquest and the exercise of arbitrary power on the part of the Government; hence, Colonel Carrington's instructions, looking mainly to the duty of selecting and building two new forts — Philip Kearney and C. F. Smith — the command assigned was only sufficient for this purpose, and for properly garrisoning the forts. This command numbered in all about seven hundred men, five hundred of whom were new recruits, and twelve officers, including district commander and staff.

The commanding officer, Colonel Carrington, did not fail to see at once, that, although his command was entirely sufficient to erect the new forts, build the barracks, warehouses, and stables, and make preparations for winter, and properly garrisoning his posts, and could protect emigration from the small thieving parties of Indians, it was still entirely inadequate to carry on a systematically aggressive war against a most powerful tribe of Indians, fighting to maintain possession and the control of their own country, in addition to those other duties.

This officer carried the orders above referred to into effect with promptness and zeal, organizing the Moun-

tain District, June 28, 1866; establishing Fort Philip
Kearney on the 15th of July, and Fort C. F. Smith
on the 3d day of August; and as early as the 31st of
July informed General P. George Cooke, the department commandant, that the status of the Indians
in that country was one of war, and requested that re-
enforcements should be sent to him. Two days previously he had telegraphed to the adjutant-general of
the army for Indian auxiliaries, and an additional
force of his own regiment.

On the 9th of August, General Cooke, commanding
the Department of the Platte, informed Colonel Carrington that Lieutenant-General Sherman ordered the
posts in his (Colonel Carrington's) district supported
as much as possible, and announced a regiment coming from St. Louis. No auxiliaries were assigned,
and no re-enforcements came until November, when
Company C, 2d United States Cavalry, reached Fort
Kearney, sixty strong, armed with Springfield rifles
and star carbines. In December, about ninety recruits joined the battalion, in the Mountain District,
a portion of whom were assigned to Company A, stationed at Fort Philip Kearney. No other re-enforcements were sent to the district.

Approved requisitions for ammunition were not
answered. The command at Fort C. F. Smith was
reduced to ten rounds per man, the command at Fort
Philip Kearney to forty-five rounds per man, and the
command at Fort Reno to thirty rounds per man.
Recruits could not practise any in firing.

Little time could be allowed from fatigue duty for drill, and, with but twelve officers and three posts, little could have been done in instructing recruits, even if time could have been allowed.

The result of all this was that the troops were in no condition to fight successful battles with Indians or other foes, and this from no fault of Colonel Carrington. It is astonishing with what zeal they fought, and the damage they inflicted on December 21st.

The numerous demonstrations and attacks made by Indians prior to the 6th of December, seemed to have been made for the sole purpose of capturing stock, picket posts, and small parties of soldiers who might venture beyond the cover of the garrison, and of annoying and checking the wood train, which was constantly drawing material for the new forts.

On the morning of December 6th, the wood train was attacked — a common occurrence — about two miles from the fort, and forced to corral and defend itself. Brevet Lieutenant-Colonel Fetterman, with a command of seventeen mounted infantry and thirty-five cavalry, moved out to relieve the wood train and to drive off the Indians. Colonel Carrington, with twenty-five mounted infantry, moved out for the purpose of cutting off the Indians from retreat and destroying them.

On this day, at a point on Reno Creek about five miles from the fort, the Indians, the second time after the fort was established, made a stand and strong resistance, and nearly surrounded Colonel Fetterman's party. The infantry obeyed orders and behaved well; the cavalry, with the exception of ten enlisted men, disobeyed the orders of Colonel Fetterman, and fled, with the greatest precipitancy, from that portion of the field.

As the cavalry retreated, the Indians made a great display and every effort to create a panic with the infantry; but Colonel Fetterman, Lieutenant Wands, and Lieutenant Brown succeeded in keeping this small body of infantry cool, and, by reserving their fire for proper range, rescued it from annihilation, effecting a junction with Colonel Carrington's party, on the east side of Reno Creek.

Lieutenant Bingham, after leaving Colonel Fetterman's party, with Lieutenant Grummond, a sergeant from Colonel Carrington's command, and two men from his own, without the knowledge or order of any of his superiors, pursued into an ambuscade, more than two miles from the main party, a single Indian, who was on foot just in front of their horses, and Lieutenant Bingham and the sergeant were there killed.

The result of this day's fighting, although not of a decidedly successful character to the Indians, was such as naturally to induce the belief on their part, that by proper management and effort they could overpower and destroy any force that could be sent out of the fort to fight them: no doubt at this time they resolved to make the effort on the first auspicious day, postponing their proceedings from the new to the full of the moon.

In the mean time, everything was quiet about the fort, although they often appeared on the surrounding hills.

On the morning of December 21st, the picket at the signal station signalled to the fort that the wood train was attacked by Indians and corralled, and the escort fighting. This was nearly 11 o'clock A. M., and the train was about two miles from the fort, moving toward the timber

Almost immediately a few Indian pickets appeared upon one or two of the surrounding heights, and a party of about twenty near the Big Piney, where the Montana road crosses the same, within howitzer range of the fort. Shells were thrown among them from the artillery in the fort, and they fled.

A detail of fifty men and two officers from the four different infantry companies, and twenty-six cavalry-men and one officer, was made by Colonel Carrington.

The entire force formed in good order, and was placed under the command of Brevet Lieutenant-Colonel Fetterman, who received the following orders from Colonel Carrington: "Support the wood train, relieve it, and report to me. Do not engage or pursue at its expense; under no circumstances pursue over Lodge-pole Ridge."

These instructions were repeated by Colonel Carrington in a loud voice, to the command when in motion, and outside the fort, and again delivered in substance by Lieutenant Wands, officer of the day, to Lieutenant Grummond, commanding cavalry detach-

15

ment, who was requested to deliver them to Colonel Fetterman.

Colonel Fetterman moved out rapidly to the right of the wood road, for the purpose, no doubt, of cutting off the retreat of the Indians thus attacking the train. As he advanced across the Piney, a few Indians appeared in his front and on his flanks, and continued flitting about him beyond rifle-range, till they disappeared beyond Lodge-pole Ridge. When he was on Lodge-trail Bridge, the picket signalled the fort that the Indians had retreated from the train; the latter train had broken corral and moved toward the timber; the train made the round trip, and was not again disturbed that day. At about fifteen minutes before twelve o'clock, Colonel Fetterman's command had reached the crest of Lodge-trail Ridge, was deployed as skirmishers, and made a halt.

Without regard to orders, for reasons that the silence of Colonel Fetterman now prevents us from giving, he, with the command, in a few moments disappeared, having cleared the ridge, still moving north.

Firing at once commenced, and increased in rapidity for about fifteen minutes, and at twelve o'clock M. there was a continuous and rapid fire of musketry distinctly heard awhile at the fort. Assistant Surgeon Hines, having been ordered to join Fetterman, found Indians on a part of Lodge-trail Ridge not visible from the fort, and could not reach the force struggling to preserve its existence. As soon as the firing

became rapid, Colonel Carrington ordered Captain
Ten Eyck, with about seventy-six men, being all the
men for duty in the fort, and two wagons with ammunition, to join Colonel Fetterman immediately. He
moved out and advanced rapidly toward the point
from which the sound of firing proceeded, but did
not move by so short a route as he might have done.
The sound of firing continued to be lessening during
his advance, diminishing in rapidity and the number
of shots till he reached a high summit overlooking
the battle-field, at about a quarter before one o'clock,
when one or two shots closed all sounds of conflict.
Whether he could have reached the scene of action, by
marching over the shortest route as quickly as possible,
in time to have relieved Colonel Fetterman's command, I am unable to determine.

Immediately after Captain Ten Eyck moved out,
and by orders of Colonel Carrington, issued at the
same time as the order detailing that officer to join
Colonel Fetterman, the quarter-master's employees,
convalescents, and all others in garrison, were armed
and provided with ammunition, being held in readiness to re-enforce the troops fighting, or to defend the
garrison.

Captain Ten Eyck reported, as soon as he reached a
summit commanding a view of the battle-field, that
the Reno Valley was full of Indians; that he could
see nothing of Colonel Fetterman's party; and requested that a howitzer should be sent to him. The
howitzer was not sent. The Indians, who, at first,

beckoned him to come down, now commenced retreating; and Captain Ten Eyck, advancing to a point
where the Indians had been standing in a circle, found
the dead, naked bodies of Brevet Lt. Colonel Fetterman, Captain Brown, and about sixty-five of the
soldiers of their command. At this point there were
no indications of a severe struggle. All the bodies
lay in a space not exceeding thirty-five feet in diameter. No empty cartridge-shells were about, and there
were some full of cartridges. A few American horses
lay dead a short distance off, all with their heads
toward the fort. This spot was by the road-side, beyond the summit of a hill, to the east of Reno Creek.
The road, after rising this hill, follows the ridge for
about half or three-quarters of a mile, then descends
abruptly to Reno Creek. At about half the distance
from where these bodies lay to the point where the
road commences to descend to Reno Creek, was the
dead body of Lieutenant Grummond; still farther on,
at the point where the road commences to descend to
Reno Creek, were the remains of the three citizens
and four or five of the old, long-tried, and experienced soldiers. A great number of empty cartridge-
shells were on the ground at this point, and more than
fifty lying on the ground about one of the dead citizens, who used a Henry rifle. Within a few hundred yards, in front of this position, ten Indian
horses lay dead, and there were sixty-five pools of
dark and clotted blood. No Indian ponies or pools
of blood were found at any other point. Our

conclusion, therefore, is that the Indians were massed to resist Colonel Fetterman's advance along Reno Creek, on both sides of the road; that Colonel Fetterman formed his advance lines on the summit of the hill overlooking the creek and valley, with a reserve. Near where the charge was made, a number of dead bodies lay; that the Indians, in a force of from fifteen to eighteen hundred warriors, attacked him vigorously in this position, and were successfully resisted by him for half an hour or more; that the command, being then short of ammunition, were seized with panic at this event, and, owing to the great numerical superiority of the Indians, attempted to retreat toward the fort; that the mountaineers and old soldiers that had learned that a movement from Indians in an engagement is equivalent to death, remained in their first position, and were killed there; that immediately upon the commencement of the retreat the Indians charged upon and surrounded the party, who could not now be formed by their officers, and were instantly killed. Only six men of the whole command were killed by balls, and two of these — Lieutenant-Colonel Fetterman and Captain Brown — no doubt, inflicted their death upon themselves, or each other, for both were shot through the left temple, and the powder was burned into the skin and flesh about the wounds. These officers had often asserted that they would not be taken alive by Indians.

Military posts have been established at various appropriate places along the emigrant roads, the North

15 *

and South Platte, Missouri and other rivers, besides among the hills, and they must be an annual expense to the United States Government of several million dollars. · Some of those forts have been excellent places of trade with the Indians, but military restrictions, in favor of sutlers, have prevented the soldiers from purchasing of other merchants, to a great extent; and have also been a disadvantage to the poor soldier, who left his home to defend the land he loved and his country's honor. The fur-trade has diminished since the war of the plains, which deters from friendly intercourse.

CHAPTER XIII.

SIOUX HISTORY — INDIAN WOMEN AND CHILDREN — SINGU-
LAR SUPERSTITION — COPPER-RIVER INDIANS — INDIAN
BEAUTY AND DECORATIONS — INDIAN PAINTING — DISGUST-
ING HABITS — SIGNS AND GESTURES.

I COMMENCE the chapter of customs and manners of Indians with a brief account of the Sioux
tribe or family, which is one of the most numerous
and powerful Indian nations upon the North American
continent; occupying all the vast territory lying
between the head-waters of the Mississippi River and
the Rocky Mountains — extending from the Arkansas
River on the south, to the shores of Lake Winnepeg
upon the north. In their career of conquest and ex-
tension, they have won for themselves renown in war
and honor in peace; their history is scarcely less
heroic than the Mohawks. When at the head of six
nations, their proud bearing and daring intrepidity
won the admiration of their enemies, and insured
their prosperity : until a comparatively short period, it
had been their boast that they had never shed the
blood of a white man.

The term Dakota signifies confederate. The nation,
consisting of seven united tribes, numbers about 28,000,
exclusive of 8,000 Assinaboines, who live west of Lake

Winnepeg. A Sioux Helen caused the separation, and the fierce encounter over this dusky beauty agitated the nation to its centre, and their feats of arms rivalled in daring and romance the Grecian exploits around the walls of Troy.

Ozalapaila, the beautiful wife of a noted chief, having fallen in love with another equally noted warrior, suffered herself to be borne away by the daring chieftain from the lodge of her husband. This was the cause of much bloodshed and suffering. Her husband and brothers having fallen in their efforts to recover her, the tribe took up the quarrel and divided, involving the whole nation in civil war; after a long and bloody struggle, the seducer and his warriors renounced their allegiance to the confederacy, and with their families retired to the north.

The divided nation has ever since been in battle upon the neutral grounds between. The family of the Sioux language is to the west of the Mississippi River what the Algonquin is to the east of that stream. Besides many affiliated tribes, the Unapaws, Osage, Kansas, Omahaw, Pawnees, Iowa, Ottoes, Missouri, and Winnebagoes, the Cheyennes, Crows, Minnetarees, Mandans, and Black Feet, all belong to this nation.

The Dakotas believe in a spirit, which they call Wakkum Tanka, and in numerous subordinate spirits, among whom the Wakkan Shecha, or evil spirit, and the Thunder are the principal, and to all these they make offerings.

These Indians have always been free from canni-
balism.   They live chiefly upon the prairies, and build
their lodges of buffalo-skins, in a conical form, so as
to permit the smoke to escape from the top, which is
left open.   They all practise polygamy, and have the
same rude notions of future life.   In a limited measure some of them cultivate the ground, raising small
quantities of maize, pumpkins, beans, squashes, and
occasionally venturing to raise a few potatoes.   Nearly
all use the dog to carry burdens, drag teepa-poles, etc.
The flesh of this animal is considered a great delicacy,
a dog-feast being regarded as a distinguished mark of
respect to a stranger.   The Winnebagoes are the only
tribe of the Sioux family found east of the Mississippi
River.   They stay in the northern part of Wisconsin,
and number about 4,500 warriors.

Indian women, although subservient in many
respects, are extremely fond of their children, over
whom they exercise a great deal of authority, as the
father scarcely ever appears to notice or exercise his
prerogative, leaving the care and control entirely in
the hands of his wife or wives; and the family is
known by the name of the wife, and not of the husband as is the case with us.   A Sioux mother binds
her baby upon a small board, wrapping it up, and
binding around it long strips of cloth, leather, or bark,
commencing at the feet and extending upward until
all but the head is enveloped; and it is only relieved
from this confined position for a few minutes at a time,
at long intervals.   In this peculiar costume it is hung

M

upon its mother's back and carried by her wherever she goes, except sometimes in her movements about the camp, when it is hung upon a projecting limb of a tree, or inclined upon the ground against the teepa, a rock, or a tree, thus permitting the mother to attend to her domestic duties. Nor is it an inappropriate condition for the child, being quite convenient for the mother, and in no wise distressing or painful to the infant, which is in this way protected from many dangerous exposures that are almost unavoidable in a wandering life. Where the camp occupies the place of kitchen, parlor, bed-room, dining-room, dog-kennel, and sometimes stable, an infant would be very much exposed if left to its own devices, or to the supervision of other children, as the mother busies herself about her domestic avocations. These consist of cooking, dressing meat for present and future use, gathering fuel, carrying water, erecting the lodges, sewing, tending the horses, saddling the ponies for the male members of the family to ride, and assisting her husband to dress himself, mount his horse, etc., while he lounges around and smokes his pipe, indifferent to the cries of his offspring, the snarling of hungry dogs under his feet, and the heavy burdens his poor wife is laboring under, considering it unmanly to contaminate his hands with any kind of menial labor, and degrading to his character as a man to thus level himself to the rank of a woman. The women practise economy in their wardrobe to rather an unpleasant extent, in not divesting themselves of their apparel until it is worn

out, thus avoiding the labor of disrobing, and of wash-
ing their clothing.

The waist and feet are never laced to diminish the
natural growth; but, which is equally as injurious to
the victim, the form of the head is, with some of
these unenlightened people, a matter of important consideration, and they endeavor to compress the skull
with a hard substance in infancy. The Flat-heads
consider a flat, retreating forehead a peculiar mark of
dignity and extraordinary beauty. The Sioux Indians, however, do not attempt to change the form of
the head at all: it is left free, and generally uncovered,
except in the most severe weather.

A Sioux woman dare not approach her husband
after the birth of a child until four weeks have tran-
spired, when the father sees his offspring for the first
time. The male children are regarded with a great
deal more interest, by all Indians, than the female,
and are always treated with more consideration and
kindness. A boy, like his father, must never be
contaminated by drudgery of any kind. To see him
lift a teepa-pole will cause his mother to lament
and wail aloud, for she, poor thing, is quite as anxious
to preserve his supremacy in this respect as his
father.

A step-father claims no authority over the children
of his wife by a former marriage, and punishment of
children by any sort of severity is extremely rare, if
it exists at all; yet for the violation of some of their
superstitious rules they punish even with death.

When the child is old enough to run alone it is relieved of its swathings, and, if the weather is not too cold, it is sent off without a particle of clothing to protect it or impede the actions of its limbs, and, in this manner, is allowed to remain until it is twelve years old, when it receives one garment. The Indian woman has some strange ideas with regard to politeness. She will never pass in front of a sachem or walk before him in a path, and will not eat out of the same dish with a man that is engaged in war, for it would degrade the brave to the level of a woman.

Great aversion is expressed by the female at finding hairs in the comb when she smooths her jetty locks; and lest some misfortune befall the finder, the loose hairs are carefully disposed of.

An Indian woman cannot be induced to cover her head. Even when removed from her savage life, she obstinately adheres to her former custom, and goes bareheaded. If a squaw wishes to climb to a higher part of the teepa than she can reach, a friendly fellow-wife or sister or daughter crouches upon the ground upon her hands and knees, offering her back for an elevator, which tender is both obliging and convenient.

An Indian woman has no rights in her own person, her husband and father being at liberty to dispose of her as their convenience dictates. Thus the hunters and trappers of the mountains are provided with wives, though the father, in selling a daughter, does not seem to relinquish his claim entirely.

Although these women are purchased at a stipulated consideration, it is no doubt a fertile source of mischief and trouble to the frontier people, as the women become fondly attached to their husbands, and naturally feel unwilling to be abandoned at their will and convenience, and left to poverty and neglect, when her only resource is to return, with her children, to the hospitality of her friends; but, be it said to the honor of that people, their hospitality is never refused to one of these unfortunate creatures.

Polygamy being believed in, and practised without restriction save by the will of the husband, and each wife being an additional honor to her husband — the women usually marry young — the husband holds his wives completely at his own mercy, even to the disposal of their lives; but with the savage, as well as with men of civilized and enlightened habits, great differences exist with individuals, and the condition of the women varies from comparative comfort to abject slavery and degradation.

Although the males regard themselves as 'infinitely superior to their females, they entertain and display a sort of respect to their wives, particularly toward the senior one, who is usually considered the ruler in the family, and generally exerts absolute authority over her associates in the teepa. Of course in this the husband is always excepted, he being supreme ruler over every member of the household.

The Sioux women, though slaves to their lords, are not quite as badly treated as their sisters on the Coppermine River, in British America, who are consid-

16

ered only property, and are subjected to most extremely brutal treatment, being used as beasts of burden, drawing loads, while their husbands and sons drive with whips, and urge the wife or mother onward with frequent applications of the lash.

These Indians, not having horses nor many dogs, make their women conveniently useful, and they are considered a source of wealth — the husband being limited in number only as regards his will and bodily strength — a man being at liberty to take the wife of any man that he can throw down; for whosoever can overcome another in wrestling, may at once seize his wife and retain her for his own, unless the former husband can succeed in throwing him down. A stout wrestler thus obtains a great many wives, whom he sometimes scantily provides for with food, and oftentimes allows those poor creatures to die of starvation, while he depends upon procuring a new supply when the times are better, by exhibiting his muscular power among his companions not so well skilled in the art of wrestling.

Much has been said of the beauty of Indian women, but observation persuades me that such tribute is an error.   If the current versions of the poet and painter be true, some blighting phenomenon had previously occurred in every instance that I saw.

Their forms are sometimes good, but their hands are large.   Their feet are usually small, and their coarse, black hair luxuriant; but such lives of exposure, drudgery, and abuse would mar the beauty of a Venus.

Some of them exhibit taste and skill in fancy work, producing some curious, if not pretty, ornaments. They are particularly skilled in the art of contriving beads tastefully, and some of their decorations in this line are truly a marvel of originality and design. They also attempt the art of painting, and display upon their teepas and buffalo-robes some designs in colors.

I saw in the hands of a mountaineer a picture of a woman and little boy, who, endeavoring to escape from an Indian camp, are being overtaken and murdered. The design was grotesque, and the coloring fearfully exaggerated, but it proved their unwillingness to acknowledge, even to themselves, that a prisoner had escaped.

It seems to be a stretch of imagination to represent an Indian woman as an artist, when we contemplate her surroundings, recalling all her unsightliness — a creature who chops wood, carries water, brings home game, skins animals, dresses hides, attends horses, secures the pony for her husband to ride, assists him to mount, and then trudges after him on foot, carrying her youngest child on her back — finally, beaten, cuffed and kicked to complete her degradation. It might be almost concluded that something by way of reform might be done for those unfortunate sisters of our own continent. It is believed that the Indian can never be enslaved, yet the Indian woman is already a slave of the worst kind, held by ignorance and love. Still, those unfortunate squaws, unlovely though they appear, have gleams of womanly kindness, dull and perverted, doubtless; but, however small, the Promethean spark glitters through the ashes of their lives. Their ideas of adornment are so much at variance with our standard of beauty, that a fully-painted squaw is a hideous monstrosity, instead of being the beautiful, attractive creature she supposes herself to be.

The countenance is variously marked with grease and paint. Sometimes the nose blooms with the hue of vermilion, the cheeks presenting a motley appearance, with black and green alternately in stripes, a star tattooed upon the forehead, and, to complete the grotesque effect, a circle of yellow drawn around each eye, which is considered the *ne plus ultra* of beauty in the toilet of a Sioux damsel, in which adornment she does not excel her brother. Not forgetting the jewelry, which is also an important addition to the general appearance, holes are cut in the rims of the ear, causing that useful organ to present an extremely uncomely appearance. Some of these apertures are so large that a finger can be thrust through, and they are filled with bits and rings of brass-wire, pieces of strings of cloth, leather, bones, etc. In the selection of jewelry, they are not governed by fashion, but each procures such as their fancy dictates and opportunity presents in their rambles or desultory trade.

Indians of both sexes wear similar blankets and

furs. It is quite difficult for a stranger to determine whether they are men or women, especially on horseback, as they all sit upon the saddle in the same way; but a person acquainted with their customs will distinguish the women at a glance, by their more miserable appearance and lower stature. They wear the hair long, yet the Osage brave wears almost no hair at all — shaving the head close to the skull, leaving, however, a small remnant.

The men are usually tall and well formed, while the female is of lower stature, and often bent with the weight of the heavy burdens she has been compelled to carry.

Many of their faults are common to both sexes — theft, vanity, laziness, drunkenness, and cruelty are predominant. Circumstances restrain some of these vices in the female, and nature adds her palliation to others. The female, in many respects, is her husband's superior.

The squaw *must* work, and all manner of labor is performed by her, except hunting, and fighting in open war, which, being considered a pleasure, she is in general denied. They all have a great fondness for spirituous liquors, and indulge freely when an opportunity presents itself; but, by a policy of the Government, their opportunities for indulging in that article are limited.

Indian women are sometimes kind and compassionate. Historians tell of several important instances where prisoners owed their thanks to Indian women
16*

for kind endeavors on their behalf; yet, to all appearances, she delights at times in bloodshed, like her husband, and will fight almost as fiercely when aroused to anger or in defence. There are not wanting instances where she has used the war-club and the tomahawk, defending her children and her honor with the fury of a lioness.

Scalping is also a pleasure when an enemy's head comes under her avenging hand, and the glory reaped by the bloody act is added to the list of her husband's achievements, when she will enter the circle of the scalp-dance, holding aloft the bloody trophy with evident satisfaction.

It is an interesting sight to the lovers of nature to see an Indian family moving. The men are all sauntering around, apparently evincing no interest whatever, or reclining upon their furs, in quiet repose, without offering to assist the over-burdened women, as they, poor souls, hasten to and fro, dragging down the lodge-poles, wrapping the tent into a compact bundle, loading the dogs and horses, packing up the cooking utensils, rolling the bedding into bundles, and, at last, when all is completed, they taking their places upon the poorest and meanest ponies, leaving their idle lords to mount the best, and, surrounded with children, dogs, bundles, and pouches, jog on, dirty, slavish, and squalid, and, it is to be hoped, contented.

The lodges are made of buffalo-skins, sewed together with sinews, in the shape of the Sibley tent used by soldiers. Indeed, it is said that the idea of the Sibley tent was suggested by the Indian teepa, and was recommended to the notice of the military authorities. These Indian teepas are variously ornamented, in proportion to the owner's taste and his position in the tribe. Every variety of colored paint is used in these decorations, and bead-work, porcupine quills, etc. Scalp-locks are portrayed upon it, indicating the number which the owner has secured. These lodges are constructed so as to be easily taken down when it is desirable to transport them to another place. They are the red man's home, and are warmer and more convenient than would be supposed. The fire being built in the centre, the smoke passes out through the aperture in the top which is made for that purpose. They are tolerably free from vermin, with the exception of lice, which belong to an Indian as unmistakably as does his swarthy color, and are as inalienable a right. Nor do they allow this seeming pest to be unprofitable, but substitute the little creatures for berries, and affirm that they are good food.

The ease with which a tent and its appointments can be packed is an advantage to their owners; for, except in the vicinity of forts, they are constantly in motion, never remaining more than a few weeks in the same place, as the Indians are compelled to follow the game for their own subsistence, and pastures for their herds. Possibly this is the reason they have no furniture. They make their beds upon the ground, and recline upon furs at their meals, where those of the same rank help themselves from the same dish,

using their fingers in place of forks. Dishes are more
common than they formerly were, as opportunities for
procuring them are greater — the emigrant trains fur-
nishing some, and traders of the country keep a good
supply for sale. Formerly they carved spoons, bowls,
etc., from roots, which was rather tedious work with
their limited supply of tools. The buffalo-horn is
still a common cup. Their arrangements at meals are
extremely unprepossessing, and in no position does an
Indian appear to a greater disadvantage than when
considered in connection with eating. The savages
appear to be utterly devoid of the delicate instincts of
appetite that distinguish humanity from the brute
creation. They consume with great relish every part
of an animal, nor do they care whether it be cooked or
raw. They will even eat carcasses of animals that
have lain dead upon the hills until the first stages of
putrefaction have appeared, and they roast small game
without freeing it of the entrails. Being very fond of
milk, they will not hesitate to procure it from dogs.
There are few animals that the Indian rejects from his
table. In this he fulfils the declaration: "Every
creature of God is good, and nothing to be refused."
It has been said that Indians will not eat the flesh of
wolves, crows, and vultures, believing the former to
be descendants of their forefathers' dogs, and, consequently, held in respect; but this is a mistaken idea.
The wolf is not good food, being too tough and
sinewy to eat; yet, when no other game can be procured,
this animal is eaten, as is also the crow and vulture,

whose flesh is usually rejected for the same reason as
is that of the wolf.

No use is made of salt, it being incovenient to procure; and they being accustomed to fresh victuals, do
not esteem it highly, believing, too, that salt has an
injurious effect upon the lungs.

Indians dry their meat in the sun, or over a fire,
and, owing to the purity of the atmosphere, it will
remain without taint, being quite palatable. The
Indians' delicacies are few, and their wants, which are
not many, are scantily supplied. As a general thing,
they are hospitably inclined. Indeed, in the intervals
of war, nothing but feasting and dancing is thought
of, and guests are received and entertained in turn at
the different lodges, with many evidences of friendship and esteem. It is customary, on entering a
friendly lodge, to carry something in the hand, if it
should be but a little bark or a pebble. Presents of
all kinds, from the most trifling up to those of value,
are made a peculiar mode of expressing friendship.
Signs and gestures are much used, and express great
meaning. In this peculiarity, Indians excel all other
people; and such is the simplicity of their signs that
they are easily learned by all who traverse the country
and make the Indian's acquaintance. These signs
might be styled the language of the plains, for the
same gestures are used by all the tribes, and, though
their language is different, they find no difficulty in
conversing intelligibly.

The Sioux, by constantly mingling with the Canadian French, who have settled among them for the purpose of trade, have learned to jabber a dialect that bears some resemblance to that language. They usually hesitate to attempt the English tongue.

From those settlers and merchants the Indians procure hatchets, knives, guns, revolvers, etc. They also barter with traders in British America, and to them sell the American horses and mules they steal from the emigrant trains as they are crossing the plains. Nor do they hesitate to drive off stock from the Government posts, from the immediate presence of the officers and soldiers, who seldom undertake to chastise the daring marauders, who have learned, in the many years of their experience, to disregard the military arm of the United States.

CHAPTER XIV.

THE Sioux Indians, like other nomadic people, are constantly changing their camps, for causes given above. The manner in which they perform these migrations is both singular and amusing. The appointment of the time is generally left to the chief of the highest rank, who intimates the hour of departure by sending criers through the village announcing his determination to move, and the hour at which he desires them to start; and, at the same time, he places his signal, which is upon his lance, on the ground, by his teepa, and by the side of it is his shield and bow.

The whole village is soon in commotion — children screaming or laughing; dogs barking and frisking; squaws running hither and thither, pulling down teepa-poles, packing up everything, and loading horses and dogs with huge burdens. The small children are placed in sacks and hung upon saddles or their mothers' backs. The usual order of arrangement is as follows: The horses and dogs are harnessed to trails; the poles of a lodge being divided into two bundles or bunches,

the small end of each is fastened upon the shoulders
or saddle of a horse, while the other end is left to
drag upon the ground, on either side; a cross-piece,
connecting the poles and keeping them in their proper
position, is attached just behind the horse ; on these
are placed the wrapped-up lodge, which is secured by
thongs, together with sundry other articles of the
household, and upon these are seated women and
children.   To guide the horse, a woman goes before,
holding the bridle, carrying on her shoulders a load
of plunder nearly as large as the horse carries upon
his back.   Women and children are sometimes
mounted upon horses, holding in their arms every
variety of plunder — sometimes little dogs, or other
forlorn pets.   In this unsightly manner, sometimes
twelve or fifteen hundred families are transported
several miles at the same migration, and, all being in
motion at the same time, the cavalcade extends for a
great distance.

The men, however, are not so unsightly in their
appearance, being mounted upon good horses, and
riding in groups, leaving the women and children to
trudge along with the burdened horses and dogs.
The number and utility of these canine assistants is
sometimes astonishing, as they count hundreds, each
bearing a portion of the general burden.   Two poles
of about twelve feet long are attached to the shoulders
of a dog, leaving one end of each dragging upon the
ground.   On these poles a small burden is carried, and
with it the faithful animal jogs along, looking neither

to the right nor to the left, but apparently intent upon reaching the end of their journey.

These faithful creatures are under the charge of squaws, and their pace is occasionally encouraged with admonitions in the form of vigorous and zealous use of willow twigs applied to their limbs and sides. It is quite amusing to see these poor animals, thus taken from their natural avocation and reduced to a life of labor, travel along with their burdens; yet, when this change has been made, they become worthless as hunters or watchers, and even for the purpose of barking, being reduced, instead, to beasts of burden. Here a great, slender hound moodily jogs along, with a frying-pan on one side and an impatient child on the other, while his companion sulks along with its own puppies suspended in a basket, and a nest of young ravens hung upon the other side. A wolfish-looking fellow toils on, supporting upon his back a piece of an antelope, buffalo, or deer, and is followed by an urchin or an old squaw, who keeps at bay all refractory companions, stimulating the memory of the loaded dogs with an occasional reminder of her presence and supremacy.

Though the Indians sail about in their canoes, they are exclusively an inland people, and aspire to no larger boats than those which may be easily paddled with the hands. These little boats are made of wood, of an oblong shape, as all readers know; but the squaws have still another boat, which suits their convenience. It is made of buffalo-skins, is almost round, and so light as to be easily transported upon the head, when they much resemble in appearance an immense black kettle turned over and put in motion; yet these small skiffs are so constructed as to be fitted to transport two persons at the same time.

The boys are early taught the arts of war. A bow and arrows are among the first presents that an Indian youth receives from his parents, and he is soon instructed in their use. Indeed, the skill of a hunter seems to be a natural endowment, and, although some are more accurate and active than others, they all shoot with wonderful precision and surprising aptitude, seeming to inherit a passionate love for the sports of the chase.

The Indian boy receives no name until some distinguishing trait of character suggests one, which is adopted, and he retains it until some other exploit or feature of character make a change necessary. He is known among white people by the literal translation of his name, as, for example: The man that stood in the water, The man who is afraid of his horses, Little Dog, Big Mouth, Red Cloud, Black Hawk, Red Jacket, etc. The girls are named from some supposed beauty, or uncomeliness, or trait of character, for example: Morning Star, White Princess, Drooping Flower, Bluebird, etc.

One of the strongest superstitions entertained by the Indian is the belief of an injurious effect to a boy that happens to be stepped over, and he will punish with great severity any one guilty of the act, considering such a movement blighting to his future growth, and impairing his strength and courage. Prisoners have sometimes offended in this way, and suffered death for their carelessness. Strange to say, the same superstitious idea does not extend to girls. The boys are taught many athletic sports, in which the youthful braves sometimes become excited to such an extent as to forget themselves and commit deeds of violence in the impetuosity of their feelings of jealousy at being outdone by opponents.

One mode of exhibiting courage is remarkably painful. It is done to prove the worthiness of an aspirant to some honorable position — possibly that of chief, or medicine-man. The brave makes a deep incision with a knife in the flesh and muscles of his chest. Into the wound thus formed he presses a short, stout stick, attached to the ends of which are two strong cords. These are secured to a tree or some other solid object. The wood being firmly fixed in the body, the aspirant uses his strength, in a backward pull, to drag it out by force. If he fails in the ordeal, he is disgraced by his want of endurance, and the position he sought for is not gained. Unless he can, on the second attempt, command more endurance, and accomplish the unnatural act, the position will be offered to another, whose fortitude may be sufficient to bear the torture.

The youths are very much addicted to war. They have no other ambition, and pant for the glory of battle, longing for the notes of the war-song, that they may rush in and win the feathers of a brave. This distinguishing mark is only worn by those who have struck an enemy's body. They listen to the tales of the old men, as they recall the stirring scenes of their youth, or sing their death-songs, which form only a boasting recapitulation of their daring and bravery. They yearn for the glory of war, which is the only path to distinction among a people who have no arts or industrial pursuits.

When a young man goes courting, he decorates himself out in his best attire, instinctively divining that appearances weigh much in the eyes of a forest belle. The young maiden receives him bashfully — for a certain kind of modesty is inherent in Indian girls, which is rather incongruous when considered in connection with their peculiar mode of life — discretion and propriety are carefully observed, and the lovers sit side by side in silence, he occasionally producing presents for her acceptance. These express a variety of sentiment, and refer to distinct and separate things, some signifying love, some friendship; others allude to the life of servitude she is expected to live, if she becomes his wife. If they are accepted graciously, and the maiden remains seated, it is considered equivalent to an assurance of love on her part, and is acted upon accordingly. Although no woman's situation is made less slavish by the marriage connection, and no one is treated with due respect, it is scarcely known in Indian life that a girl has remained single even to middle age — which, by the way, is not a surprising truth, when we look back one century upon our own race, and consider, in all its connections, the position of the white woman.

When an attachment has progressed very far, the lovers will each comb the other's jetty locks, and compliment their beauty; but this is when marriage is contemplated, and the preliminaries are arranged. Except when contaminated with civilized influences by association and example, the Indians respect decorum, and marriage is regarded an honorable institution; and such is their horror of unchaste conduct, that death has not unfrequently been the penalty. An incident of that kind was related by an eye-witness:

A young girl was tried for unchaste conduct, and found guilty, and was condemned to suffer death. She was taken to a spot beyond the village, and, in the presence of the band, executed. Her seducer chanted her death-song, as she came calmly forward, and knelt down in the centre of the circle, and covered her head. While the song and the noise of a drum sounded loudly, a warrior silently approached the kneeling figure, and gave one rapid stroke of his tomahawk. She sank at his feet upon the ground. "It is better for her to die, and go to the happy hunting-grounds," they said, "than to live a life of dishonor and shame among her own people."

Their reverence for the marriage ceremony is illustrated in the following story:

A gentleman, who was a commissioned officer of

17 *

the Iowa volunteers, fell in love with an Indian girl, and desired to make her his wife — not by the Indian custom, but according to the laws of the land. This girl, who lived among the hills, and had never visited a fort before, was educated purely in Indian fashion. Her father gave his consent, and at the fort they were married by the chaplain; but this ceremony was to the ignorant maiden utterly meaningless, nor could even her father persuade her of its legality, and she refused even to look at her husband, who, not understanding her prejudice, feared she had been influenced through coercion to become his wife, but was assured by her father that no persuasions had been used; and, as the girl could not speak in English, the cause of her grief was peculiarly mysterious to the young officer, who had supposed she would be happy. He endeavored to convince her of his love, and to awaken a corresponding degree of regard in her bosom. Finally he resorted to every device that knowledge of Indian character could suggest to his mind. He bought her clothes, fruits, wines, etc., engaged handsome rooms, supplied them with costly furniture, and introduced pleasant company. All her presents she religiously divided with her parents, in this way spoiling everything he gave her; for it was not to give one of two articles, but the half of each. Thus all the bottles of wine were opened, as was each can of fruit, and all her dress patterns were divided into two pieces.

Some months before, a wealthy chief had offered his son, whom she had accepted, but her father interfered,

and, though twenty ponies were brought to his door
as a price for his daughter, he refused to let her go,
his ambition being to see her the wife of a white man,
and now a white man had married her; but she was
not a happy wife.   Three days she sat upon the floor,
veiled and in silence, to the utter surprise of every
person, and the grief and discouragement of her husband, who feared she loved the young Indian her
father had rejected.   Finally, however, in answer to
his repeated inquiries, she told him she was her
mother's child, and not his wife; for he had given
nothing to her father for her.

Very joyfully the young husband sprang away in
quest of a horse, which he presented to the bride's
father, thus quite satisfying her scruples and making
her happy, as well as himself, for he was relieved to
know that his wife's misery was caused only by the
nonfulfilment of a native ceremony.

I am persuaded that the·squaw is a slave to her
husband and father through the influence of coercion,
because when she is married to a white man she claims
her rights, and obstinately insists upon having them.
In resignation and ignorance she serves her Indian
lord, without ever dreaming of any reform in her
hard lot.

When the body of an enemy is found, the honor of
having killed the person is bestowed upon the finder,
even if the deceased has died naturally, and the body
lain for months in its decaying condition.   If a woman
finds the body of a person, the glory passes over to her
husband.

When Indians are pursued closely, they evince a desperate and reckless desire to save themselves, without regard to friends or property. Mothers will throw away their infants when they impede their flight, and all instinct seems lost but that of fear. In an attack, the post of fame consists in the distinction of being foremost.

Scalping, to the Indian, is a surgical rapture, which he performs with a dexterity and aptitude proving his love for the art. The left hand grasps the hair, and a few well-directed strokes of the knife separate the skin from the head; then the memento of victory is carefully preserved and exhibited to increase the enthusiasm and valor in the hearts of the young men. Indeed, the effect upon the minds of their youth seems to be the object of nearly all the hateful ceremonies of Indian amusements.

Dancing is very much practised among the Sioux Indians, as well as among all other barbarous people. In dancing, the Sioux have several distinct religious ceremonies — the scalp dance, corn dance, bull dance, war dance, pipe or peace dance, etc. The scalp dance is given in celebration of a victory, and is always performed in the night by the light of huge fires or torches. When a war party returns from a foraging expedition, bringing home in triumph scalps of an enemy, those that feel inclined to rejoice collect together in a circle. The braves come vauntingly forth with the most extravagant boasts of their wonderful powers and courage in war, at the same time

brandishing weapons in their hands with the most
fearful contortions and threatenings. A number of
young women are generally selected to aid, though
they do not actually join in the dance; however, if
they feel like dancing, the privilege is not denied
them; but it is their duty to hold aloft the scalps,
while the warriors jump around in a circle brandishing their weapons, and barking and yelping in a most
frightful manner, all jumping upon both feet at the
same time, with simultaneous stamping and motions
with their weapons, keeping exact time. Their gestures impress one as if they were actually cutting and
carving each other to pieces as they utter their sharp,
short yelps. They become furious as they grow more
excited, until each face is distorted to the utmost; their
glaring eyes protrude with a fiendish, indescribable appearance, while they snap and grind their teeth, and
the white foam gathers around their mouths, and they
actually breathe through their inflated nostrils the
hissing sound of death in battle. Furious and faster
grows the stamping, until the sight is more like a picture of fiends in a carnival of battle, than anything
else to which the scene can be compared. No description can fully convey the terrible sight in all
its fearful barbarity, as the bloody trophies of their
victory are brandished aloft in the light of the flicker-
ing blaze, and their distorted forms are half concealed
by darkness.

Frantically seizing imaginary victims, they affect
to execute in furious excitement the most fiendish

torture upon them, while the air is filled with the sound of their yelps and screams.

The precise object for which the scalp is taken is exultation, and proof of valor and success; but the motive for this ceremony is a subject not yet satisfactorily settled among those who have studied the Indian character.

There is no doubt but one object is public exultation, yet there is conclusive evidence that there are other and weighty motives for thus formally displaying the scalp. Mr. Catlin says among some tribes it is customary to bury the scalps after this public exhibition, which has, to a certain extent, been held for the purpose of giving them notoriety and of awarding public credit to the person or persons who obtained the scalps, and from a custom of the tribe who are about to part from them forever. The respect which is paid to scalps while they are in the Indians' possession, as well as the mournful songs which they howl to the memory of their unfortunate victims, with the precise care and solemnity with which they afterward bury the scalp, sufficiently convinces him that they have a superstitious dread of the spirits of their slain enemies, and believe they have certain conciliatory offices to perform to insure their own peace.

CHAPTER XV.

THE Bull Dance is one of the greatest religious ceremonies of the Mandans, and one through which every young man must pass before he is admitted to the dignity of a brave. These rites are held annually, and are looked forward to with much interest.

The great mystery-lodge is opened, strewn with herbs and boughs, and adorned with buffalo and human skulls. During the first day, a mysterious person known as the first and only man, passes from one lodge to another, relating what has happened on the surface of the earth by the overflowing of the waters, affirming that he was the only person saved from that fearful calamity; that he landed his big canoe on a high mountain in the west, where he now resides; that he had come to open the medicine-lodge, which must need presents in the shape of edged tools from the owner of every lodge, that they may be sacrificed to the spirit of the waters. If this is not done, there will be another flood, and none will escape its destruction, as it was with such tools that the big canoe was made. The implements are always given and deposited in the medicine-lodge. During the night no one is able to ascertain where the strange being sleeps, and silence reigns through the village. On the following morning he again appears, followed by the young men candidates for the ordeal, who enter with this mysterious person into the medicine-lodge, where they remain four days, praying and fasting, and holding no communication with outsiders. Meanwhile the bull dance takes place in the village. Catlin thus describes the scene:

"This very curious and exceedingly grotesque part of their performance — one of the avowed objects for which they hold this annual *fête*, and to the strict observance of which they attribute the coming of the buffaloes to supply them with food during the approaching season — is repeated four times during the first day, eight times on the second, twelve times on the third, and sixteen times on the fourth day, and always around the curb, or 'big canoe,' of which I have spoken.

"The principal actors in it are eight men, with the entire skins of buffaloes thrown over their backs, the horns, hoofs, and tails remaining on: their bodies being in a horizontal position, enables them to imitate the actions of the buffalo. They look out through the apertures of its eyes, as through a mask.

"The bodies of these men are chiefly naked, and all painted in the most extraordinary manner, with the nicest adherence to exact similarity; their limbs, bodies, and faces being in every part covered, either with black, red, or white paint. Each one of these

strange characters has also a lock of buffalo's hair
tied around his ankle, and in his right hand a rattle,
and a slender white rod or staff, six feet long, in the
other. Each one carries upon his back a bunch of
green willow boughs about the usual size of a sheaf of
wheat. These eight men divide into four pairs, and
take their positions on the four different sides of the
curb or big canoe, representing thereby the four cardinal points. Between each group of them, with the
back turned to the big canoe, is another figure, engaged in the same dance, keeping step with them, with
a similar staff or wand in one hand, and a rattle in the
other, and (being four in number) answering again
to the four cardinal points.

"The bodies of these four young men are chiefly
naked, with no other dress upon them than a beautiful kilt or quartz-quaw around the waist, made of
eagles' quills and ermine, and very splendid head-
dresses of the same materials. Two of these figures
are painted entirely black with pounded charcoal and
grease, and they are called the 'firmament, or night;'
the numerous white spots which are dotted all over
their bodies are called 'stars.' The other two are
painted from head to foot as red as vermilion can
make them. These, they say, represent the day, and
the white streaks which are painted up and down over
their bodies are ghosts, which the morning rays are
chasing away

"This most remarkable scene, which is witnessed
more or less often each day, takes place in the pres-
18

ence of the whole nation, who are gathered around on the tops of the wigwams or other places as spectators, while the young men are reclining and fasting in the lodge as above described. On the first day this *'bull dance'* is given *once* to each of the cardinal points, and the medicine-man smokes his pipe to those directions; on the second day, *twice* to each; *three times* to each on the third day, and *four times* to each on the fourth. As a signal for the dancers and other characters (as well as the public) to assemble, the old man, master of ceremonies, with the medicine-pipe in hand, dances out of the lodge, singing, or rather crying forth a most pitiful lament, until he approaches the big canoe, against which he leans, with a pipe in hand, and continues to cry. At this instant four very aged and patriarchal-looking men, whose bodies are painted red, and who have been guarding the four sides of the lodge, enter it and bring out four sacks of water, which they place near the big canoe, where they seat themselves by the side of them, and commence striking on the sacks with mallets or drum-sticks, which have been lying on them; and another brandishes and shakes the eeh-na-dees, or rattles. All unite with them, their voices raised to the highest pitch possible, as the music for the bull dance, which is then commenced and continued for fifteen minutes or more in perfect time, without cessation or intermission. When the music and dancing stop, which is simultaneous, the whole nation raise a deafening shout of approbation, the master of ceremonies dances back to the medicine-lodge, and the old men return to their former places. The sacks of water and all rest as before, until, by the same method, they are again called into a similar action.

" The supernumeraries who play their parts in this grand spectacle are numerous, and well worth description. By the side of the big canoe are seen two men, with the skins of grisly bears thrown over them, using the skins as a mask over their heads. These ravenous animals are continnally growling, and threatening to devour everything before them interfering with the forms of their religious ceremony. To appease them, the women are continually bringing and placing before them dishes of meat, which are as often snatched up and carried to the prairie by two men, whose bodies are painted black and their heads white, whom they call bald eagles, who are darting by them, and grasping their food from before them as they pass. These are again chased upon the plains by a hundred or more small boys, who are naked, their bodies painted yellow and their heads white, whom they call *cabris* or antelopes, who at length get the food away from them and devour it, thereby inculcating (perhaps) the beautiful moral that by the dispensations of Providence 'His bountiful gifts will fall at last to the hands of the innocent.'

" During each and every one of these dances, the old men, who beat upon the sacks and sing, are earnestly chanting forth their supplications to the Great Spirit for the continuation of his influence in sending them buffaloes to supply them with food during the year, and are inculcating admiration of courage and fortitude to the young men in the lodge, by telling them that the Great Spirit has opened his ears in their behalf — that the very atmosphere all about them is peace — that their women and children can hold the mouth of the grisly bear — that they have invoked from day to day O-ke-hee-de (the evil spirit) — that they are still challenging him to come, and yet he has not dared to make his appearance. But, alas! at last, on the fourth day, in the midst of all their mirth and joy, and about noon, when they are in the height of all their exultation, a sudden scream bursts from the tops of the lodges — men, women, dogs, and all seem actually to howl and shudder with alarm, as they fix their glaring eyeballs upon the prairie bluffs, about a mile in the west, down the side of which a man is seen descending at full speed toward the village.   This strange character darts about in a zigzag course in all directions on the prairie, like a boy in pursuit of a butterfly, until he approaches the pickets of the village, when it is discovered that his body is entirely naked, and painted as black as a negro with pounded charcoal and bear's grease.   His body is, therefore, everywhere of a shining black, except occasional white rings, of an inch or more in diameter, which are marked, here and there, all over him; and frightful representations of canine teeth around his mouth adding to his hideous appearance as he utters the most frightful shrieks and screams, dashes through the village, and enters the terrified group which is composed (in that quarter) chiefly of females, who have assembled to witness the amusements which were transpiring around the 'big canoe.' This unearthly creature carries in his hands a wand or staff, eight or nine feet in length, with a red ball at the end of it, which he continually slides on the ground before him as he runs. All eyes in the village, save those of the persons engaged in the dance, are centred upon him. He makes a desperate rush toward the women, who scream for protection as they endeavor to retreat — falling in groups upon each other in their struggles to get out of his reach. In this moment of general terror and alarm there is an instant check, and all for a few moments are as silent as death.

"The old master of ceremonies, who has run from his position at the big canoe, has met this monster of fiends, and, having thrust the medicine-pipe before him, holds him still and immovable under his charm. This check gives the females an opportunity to get out of his reach. When they are free from this danger, though all hearts beat with the sudden excitement, their alarm soon cools down into the most extravagant laughter and shouts of applause, at his sudden defeat, and at the awkward and ridiculous posture in which he was stopped and held. The old man was braced stiff by his side, with his eyeballs glaring in his face, while the medicine-pipe held in its mystic chains his Satanic Majesty, annulling all the powers of his magical wand, and also depriving him of the power

18 *   O

of locomotion. Surely no two human beings ever presented a more striking group than these two individuals do for a few moments, with their eyeballs set in mutual hatred, defying each other; both struggling for the supremacy, relying on the potency of their medicine or mystery — the one held in check, with his body painted black, representing (or rather assuming to be) his sable majesty, O-ke-hee-de, (the evil spirit,) frowning vengeance on the other, who sternly gazes back with a look of exultation and contempt, as he holds him in check, disarming the enemy. The charm of his mystic pipe (on the power of which hangs all these annual mysteries) has been thus fully tested and acknowledged, and the women have had, by its means, sufficient time to escape from this fiendish monster.

" The pipe is very gradually withdrawn from before him, and he seems delighted to recover the use of his limbs again, with the power of changing his position from the exceedingly unpleasant and ridiculous one he so lately appeared in, and was compelled to maintain a few moments before. He was rendered more superlatively ridiculous and laughable from the further information I am constrained to give of the plight in which this demon of terror makes his *entrée* into the village and to the centre and nucleus of their first and greatest religious ceremony.

" In this plight he pursues the groups of females, spreading dismay and alarm wherever he goes, and consequently producing the awkward and exceedingly laughable predicament in which he is placed by the sudden check from the medicine-pipe, as I have above stated.   When all eyes are intently fixed upon him, and all join in rounds of applause for the success of the magic spell that is placed upon him, all voices are raised in shouts of satisfaction at his defeat, and all eyes gaze upon him — of chiefs and warriors, matrons, and even of their tender - aged and timid daughters, whose education had taught them to receive the *morale* of these scenes without the shock of impropriety that would have startled a more fastidious, and, consequently, sensual-thinking people.

"After repeated attempts thus made and thus defeated in several parts of the crowd, this blackened monster is retreating over the ground where the buffalo dance is going on, and, having swaggered against one of the men placed under the skin of a buffalo, and engaged in the bull dance, he starts back, and places himself in the attitude of a buffalo.   After this he pays his visits to three others of the eight, in succession, receiving, as before, the deafening shouts of approbation which peal from every mouth in the multitude, who are all praying to the Great Spirit to send them buffaloes to supply them with food during the season, attributing the coming of buffaloes for this purpose entirely to the strict and critical observance of this ridiculous and disgusting part of the ceremony. During the half-hour or so that he has been jostled about among the men and beasts, to the great amusement and satisfaction of the lookers-on, he seems to have become suddenly exceedingly alarmed, anxiously looking out for some feasible mode of escape. In this awkward predicament he becomes the laughing-stock and butt for the women, who, no longer afraid, are gathering in groups around, to tease and tantalize him. In the midst of this dilemma, which soon becomes a very sad one, one of the women steals up behind him, with both hands full of yellow dirt, and dashes it into his face and eyes and all over him; and his body, being covered with grease, takes instantly a different hue. He seems heart-broken at this disgrace, and commences crying most bitterly, when another catches his wand from his hand, and breaks it across her knee. It is snatched for by others, who break it still into bits, and throw them at him. His power is now gone — his bodily strength exhausted, and he starts for the prairie. He dashes through the crowd, and makes his way through the pickets on the back part of the village, where are placed, for the purpose, a hundred or more women and girls, who follow him, as he runs on the prairie, for half a mile or more, beating him with sticks, stones, and dirt, and giving him kicks and cuffs, until he is at length seen escaping from their grasp, and making the best of his retreat over the prairie bluffs, whence he first appeared. This terminates the bull dance, one of the most sacred institutions of the Mandan Sioux."

Mr. Bollar gives a graphic account of the bull dance, as practised among the Indians of his acquaint-

ance, which is more barbarous than religious or indi-
cative of courage.   I give an extract:

"On the third day of the dance, two old warriors
emerged from the medicine-lodge, closely followed by
two young men.   Going up to two stout poles, about
twelve feet high, firmly planted in the ground, they
disengaged cords of raw hide hanging from them.
One of the young men knelt at the foot of the pole,
resting his thighs on his heels, and, throwing his head
back and his breast forward, supported himself in this
position by his hands.   The old men now, one on either
side, with a common butcher-knife cut through the
skin and flesh on each breast, and thrust splinters
under the sinews, attaching the thongs to them.   The
other young man was quickly served in the same way.
Not a muscle of their countenances moved, and not a
sound escaped their lips while this painful operation
was in progress.   Each rose to his feet, and, throwing
the whole weight of his body upon the cords, while
the blood streamed from the wounds, tried to tear
himself loose.   One, as soon as he was left alone,
sprang wildly to the full length of the cord, and then,
hanging with his entire weight upon the sinews of his
breast, swung back, striking the posts violently.

"Again and again he swung himself off, and around
the pole, calling, in the most agonizing tones, to the
Great Spirit, and praying that he might hereafter be
a successful warrior and hunter, and that his heart
might be 'made strong,' to enable him to bear his
present sufferings.   After being self-tortured in this

way for some time, he fainted, and hung, to all appearance, as though dead.

"The strain on the splinters finally tore them out, and he fell to the ground, when his relatives came forward and took him in charge, carrying him off to a lodge, where, after he revived, food would be given to him, and he might then receive the congratulations of his friends.

"The other youth uttered not a word, though he was quite young — not more than eighteen years old — and for some time walked around the pole, shrinking from the fearful test. At last, having nerved himself up to it, he suddenly swung off with all his strength, and, returning, struck the post with such violence that he also fainted, and hung, a sickening, pitiable sight, with the blood streaming from his self-inflicted wounds.

"In no instance can the splinter be pulled out; for, to do so would be fatal to the anticipated beneficial result. In cases where the sinews are very strong, it becomes necessary to add weights to the person, as his own weight and exertions may prove insufficient for the task. All who can pass through this ordeal are regarded as brave men, strong-hearted warriors and hunters.

"The fourth or closing day was mostly a repetition of the third. Those of the young men who had not succeeded in tearing themselves loose from the poles, were dragged in a circle by the hands, until the buffalo-skulls or other weights that had been fastened to their legs were torn off by the violence of the race; and it has happened, more than once, that the tough sinews, defying every effort to break them, rendered it necessary for the unfortunate sufferer to crawl off on the prairie, and there remain until it had rotted completely out."

CHAPTER XVI.

THE Indians' organs of sight and hearing are cultivated to a degree of perfection that sometimes leads persons to associate the supernatural with their sagacity in detecting sounds and appearances. It is, however, only the natural result of continuous, careful training; and trappers of the Rocky Mountains are said to be equally as apt in the use, if they do not excel the Indian in the exquisite fineness of these particular senses.

When not in immediate danger, the men are quite unguarded in their travels; and as they have no commissaries, but depend upon the game they can procure, they usually separate to hunt, and travel, through the day, in small companies, always arriving at a designated place for their night encampment.

They understand the rising and setting of the moon, and watch the stars when they travel at night. They name many of the constellations. The Sioux have a legend about the morning star, which is rather peculiar. They believe it was once a lovely damsel, who pined for the company of the sun, and longed to go to the land from whence comes the daylight. Her brother, a great chieftain, was anxious that her wish should be gratified, and, by an invocation to the Great Spirit, Wakkun Tanka, succeeded in raising a storm of wind that came from the four corners of the earth, and she was borne away in it, and placed beside the sun. In love and remembrance of her people, she comes each morning to warn them of the approaching day.

Indians seldom indulge in outcry or invective: considering submission to the inevitable a virtue, they practise it quietly, seeming to depart this life, even by execution, without malice or desire for revenge. When they are convinced that death cannot be postponed, they prepare to meet it with a stoical indifference, which reminds one of the Hindoo under similar circumstances, and seems to be a part of the fatalism that constitutes the bulwark of all savage superstition and religion. They seem to evince philosophy and dignity at this trying hour, which peculiar feature of character has won the admiration of many persons, who have witnessed their death by execution. The Indian women are exceptions to this rule, for they, unlike the men, make outcry a virtue, and indulge in it to excess; sometimes putting ashes, or other irritating substances, in their eyes, to cause tears, when sorrow fails to produce them. At the death of a friend, it is the duty of the squaws to wail aloud, while at the death of a chieftain the air is filled with the sound of their wailing voices.

19

The chieftainship is not hereditary, although the eldest son of his highness is respected as an under chief in honor of his father's power, during his parent's lifetime. To obtain the position of leading chief among the Sioux, the warrior must perform some personal feat of bravery or endurance entitling him to honor in the opinion of the tribe. Besides the head chief, they have leaders corresponding to captains, lieutenants, etc., who are selected without regard to position, but for good judgment and discretion, and are usually skilled in all matters of custom and counsel.

The medicine-man is generally considered next to the first chief in rank, and sometimes exercises great authority and peculiar skill. He is prophet, physician, and teacher, though the supernatural power of vision is not exclusively confined to him; for all the aged men believe they are endowed with that gift, and are firm believers in dreams and the gift of prophecy. The medicine-men depend upon herbs, sweats, laying-on of hands, etc., and many instances of remarkable cure are reported to have been effected through their influence and skill, and it is an undisputed fact in the annals of botanic medicine, that the herbs most in esteem in our country are the result of disclosures on the part of the aborigines.

Their surgery, however, is lamentably deficient. They place much reliance upon charms and incantations. Their knowledge is limited and their practice unfortunate. For instance, a case of swollen tonsils, of obstinate character, an Indian doctor attempted to cure; and when mild means had failed, he seized the palate with a pair of bullet-moulds, tearing the mouth and throat fearfully, and causing death.

Severe wounds are sometimes inflicted upon the sick to dislodge evil spirits supposed to be lurking around to the disadvantage of the afflicted person.

Small-pox, and all other contagious diseases, they hesitate to attempt to cure, and those who are attacked generally resign themselves to a state of apathy, making no effort to stay the progress of a direful malady, and sometimes great numbers of them die in a very short time. This I believe to be one cause of the decline of that people. Surely it is not, as is so generally supposed, the intrusion of the white people into their country, for they still have a superabundance of territory.

The cause of their decline as a nation has been inquired of me; but a positive answer to this question is beyond my ability to give; yet, it is my opinion that a correct answer to the question is indolence and ignorance, which definition, however, extends over a vast area, when their whole character and lives are considered.

Sometimes the medicine-man attempts to cure diseases by incantations, swinging a rattle, and chanting a song; and, at the same time, he is adorned with the emblems of his art, which are arranged upon his person, for the purpose of impressing the mind of the patient with the marvellous. Really the entire operation is, to a certain extent, mesmerization, or a sort of charm. Not unlike his brother physicians in civilized communities, the Indian doctor endeavors to confound the people by an unintelligible language, and serious expressions of countenance, as a substitute for real knowledge and skill, thus concealing his incompetency under the disguise of learning, sometimes to the destruction of his confiding patient.

Though Indians in all sections adhere to their own faith, the Mexicans offer an example of a change of religion; yet it was not by conviction or conversion, but by coercion.

An instance is recorded of Pizarro, the conqueror of Peru, in his invasion of that country, meeting the Inca Atahualpa, and endeavoring to convince the monarch of his error in religion. A friar, with more zeal than piety, advanced to the Peruvian inca, with a crucifix in one hand and a Bible in the other, and, in a loud voice, began a formal discourse, explaining the history of the creation of the world, the fall of man, the doctrine of the incarnation, the death and resurrection of Jesus Christ — in brief, a summary of the contents of the Bible.

The barbarian chief listened to all with composure, until the harangue was finished, when he ventured to expostulate, saying: "It would be foolish and impious in me to change my religion, which has been transmitted to me by my ancestors, until I am convinced that mine is false and yours is true. You worship a God that died on a tree; for my part, I adore the sun, that never dies. As to the story of the creation and the fall of man, how did you learn it?" "In this book," cried the enraged priest. Seizing the book, the monarch held it to his ear. "This book," said he, "tells me nothing," and he contemptuously threw it upon the ground. This disbelief, and disrespect for the Holy Book, was a pretext for slaughter, and the Spanish soldiers, filled with religious bigotry, covered the ground with murdered bodies of the Peruvians, and their own name with disgrace and shame.

The Northern Indians have at all times tenaciously adhered to their own faith, and have expressed a great antipathy to the doctrines of Christianity. Although attempts have been repeatedly made to Christianize them, they have been futile, or attended with but little success, and oftentimes the result has been the reverse of the anticipated benefit, and still further degradation in morals has followed these endeavors. Those whose experience has been the most extensive and varied, testify to the fact that the wild Indian is much superior to his half-civilized brother, both in morality and sentiment.

Red Jacket expressed his opinion upon religion in reply to a missionary who came to instruct him in the doctrines of the Bible, and it may not be inappropriate to insert it in this connection:

"Friends and brothers, it is the will of the Great Spirit that we should meet together this day. He orders all things, and has given us a fine day for the council. He has taken His garments from before the

19 *

sun and caused it to shine with brightness upon us. Our eyes are opened that we see clearly — our ears are unstopped that we have been able to hear the words that you have spoken. For these favors we thank the Great Spirit, and Him only.

"Brothers, this council-fire was kindled by you. It is at your request that we come together at this time. We have listened with attention to what you have said. You requested us to speak our minds' freely. This gives us great joy; for we now consider that we stand upright before you, and can speak what we think. All have heard your voice, and all speak to you as one man. Our minds are agreed.

"Brothers, you say you want an answer to your talk before you leave this place. It is right that you should have one, as you are a great distance from home, and we do not wish to detain you; but we will first look back a little, and tell you what our fathers have told us, and what we have heard from the white people.

"Brothers, you say you are sent to instruct us how to worship the Great Spirit agreeably to His mind, and if we do not take hold of this religion which you white people teach, we shall be unhappy hereafter. You say you are right, and we are wrong. How do we know this to be true? We understand that your religion is written in a book. If it was intended for us as well as you, why did not the Great Spirit give it to us, and not only to us, but to our forefathers; also the means of understanding it rightly? We only know what you tell about it. How shall we know when to believe, having been so often deceived by white people?

"Brothers, you say there is but one way to worship and serve the Great Spirit. If there is but one religion, why do you white people differ so much about it? Why not all agree, as you can all read the book?

"Brothers, we do not understand these things. We are told that your religion was given to your forefathers, and has been handed down from father to son. We also have a religion which was given to our forefathers, and has been handed down to us, their children. We worship this way. It teacheth us to be thankful for all the favors we receive, to love each other, and to be united. We never quarrel about religion.

"Brothers, the Great Spirit made us all, but He has made a great difference between his red and white children. The Great Spirit does right. He knows what is best for His children. We are satisfied.

"Brothers, we do not wish to destroy your religion, or take it from you; we only want to enjoy our own.

"Brothers, we have been told that you have been preaching to the white people. We will wait a little while, and see what effect your preaching has upon them. If we find it does them good, we will consider. If it makes them honest, and less disposed to cheat Indians, we will then consider again what you have said.

"Brothers, you have now heard our answer to your talk, and this is all we have to say now. As we are going to part, we will come and take you by the hand, and we hope the Great Spirit will protect you on your journey, and return you safe to your friends."

Mingled with much truth in their religion is an undercurrent of superstition, which contaminates the simplicity of their belief with deformity and crime. I quote an instance from Schoolcraft:

"The Iowa Indians, having taken prisoner a Sioux girl of fourteen years of age, resolved to sacrifice her to the Great Spirit, or rather the Spirit of Corn. For this purpose she was placed upon a foot-rest, between two trees, about two feet apart, and raised above the ground just high enough to allow a torturing fire to be built under her feet. Here she was held by two warriors, who mounted the rest beside her, and applied lighted torches and splinters under her arms. At a given signal, a hundred arrows were discharged into her body. These were immediately withdrawn, and her flesh was cut from the bones, in small pieces, which they placed in baskets, and carried into the corn-field, where they squeezed a little blood into each hill."

Another instance of their barbarous superstition is told by an eye-witness:

"In the summer of 1861, a party of Sac and Fox Indians returned to their reservation from a hunt in the Arkansas River country, in which they had been unusually unsuccessful, and, divining the cause of their misfortuncs to be lurking in the person of an old woman, they resolved to clear their tribe of the harbored evil spirits, which caused them to suffer by being unfortunate in the chase.

"A council was held to determine the mode of her death, where it was decided that she should be shot, and the body afterward burned to ashes, which would destroy the devils or other malicious spirits which infested it.

"This decision was immediately carried into effect, and the poor old woman, who did not doubt the wisdom of the councillors, nor offer to remonstrate against the decree that decided her fate, was led beyond the village and executed. It was truly a pitiable sight, to see her sad countenance, and bowed and trembling form, as she was taken from her home forever. As she emerged from the door, her daughter — an only child and sole remaining friend — stepped forward with a sorrowful yet resigned look upon her countenance, and placed her own best robe around her trembling form, with the only words, 'My mother!' She was superstitious as the rest, yet a daughter's love still lingered in her breast; and though it might be death to sympathize, her sorrow was apparent.

"After this barbarous ceremony was completed, there was a season of rejoicing and hilarity, in which time they indulged freely in copious libations of spirituous liquors of the most poisonous character, which, in the opinion of the observer, contained more evil spirits — if a conclusion could be arrived at by its apparent

P

influence upon their behavior — than could possibly have been confined in the victim of their barbarous superstition."

All heathen people are superstitious, yet some to a greater extent than others. An Indian will not sacrifice his own life for his religion: it is more congenial to his idea of propriety to sacrifice another's. Nor do the American Indian women offer as liberally as some other barbarians do: for example, the Mogul women offer themselves to the flames, at the death of their husbands; and there are others who immolate their children to their gods. Yet the squaw believes in punishing self, and making great outward display of grief on the death of a friend.

" When other means to procure buffalo fail, a white flag is hoisted, bearing a rude painting, in vermilion, of the sun and moon, to which they make offerings. An Indian walks in a circle around the place all day, crying and praying to the Great Spirit to grant them success in war and the chase. Near by is a small pile of human skulls. Around each of these is bound a cloth of bright color. The lance is thrust into the ground beside them, supporting his shield and medicine-pouch. During the period he spends in this supplication, he does not eat, nor speak to any one, lest the spell be broken, and the great anticipated benefit be lost."

Their sacrifices are evidences of the savage's faith in God. The Sioux Indians are a religious people, so far as their knowledge of Christianity extends.

Though they do not understand the teachings of the Holy Word as given to us by inspiration, they have a reverence for a Supreme Ruler, and a superstitious fear of the wrath of a Bad Spirit. Some of their sacrifices are offered to the Bad Spirit; for they believe it is safest not to incur his wrath. The Good Spirit they believe is too good to do them an injury, but that it is the Evil Spirit who causes their misfortunes.

A dance called the buffalo dance is practised. A medicine-man is supposed to have a vision regarding the season for the buffalo dance, which is apt to be when the buffalo are scarce but still expected; and soon after he goes to a huge butte, or other elevation, and begins a cry and prayer to the Great Spirit. This he continues to do for three days, fasting all the while. At the expiration of that time the buffalo are looked for, from the greatest eminences of the neighborhood. Silence is observed as much as possible during the three days. An unlucky squaw who happens to forget herself, and undertakes to chop wood, is sure to receive a sound beating. Travel and hunting are also forbidden during this time, and even conversation is avoided.

If this medicine brings the buffalo, the dreamer receives a valuable present; if not, the dance is commenced, and continued until they do appear.

The Indians' amusements are varied in character, as circumstances require. Dancing is much practised, and the smoke dance — an expression of savage feeling, yet of kindness to each other — ranks among the most innocent of their amusements. It is performed under peaceful influences, and is ceremonious and stately in character. The Indian women do not smoke, but they prepare bark, which they procure from the red willow, and substitute for tobacco, and they get the pipes in order, etc.

A fire is lighted beyond the village as preliminary, and around it the dancers, who are usually young men, assemble, and seat themselves upon robes of buffalo-skins. A chief or medicine-man presides, and, with a long-stemmed pipe in his right hand, bows to the east, west, north, and south, saying, "Take it, Great Spirit, and smoke," and, at the same time, he offers the pipe to each of the cardinal points, thus invoking the co-operation of the good spirits. All believe, when this is done, that they are in league with the spirits of good and evil, and the pipe is passed around, each one making a few puffs. The chief then begins a song in a low, monotonous tone, while the next in rank beats upon a drum, and accompanies his movements with a song, differing altogether from the other.

Under the inspiration of this combined song or harmony, a brave leaps up and cuts a few capers, bounding and jumping to the taps of the drum; then seizing a companion by the hand, he drags him to the centre of the circle, where they flourish around. The second dancer soon catches the hand of another companion, who, in turn, seizes another, and the performance is continued until the circle of dancers is complete, when they all dance in unison.

Their movements are at first graceful, but they soon become animated, and, as the dance progresses, they grow excited, their movements then being wild and grotesque. They leap, and fling themselves about with reckless abandon, shaking their fists in each other's faces, mimicking the barking and growling of dogs, contorting their features in a shocking manner, making grotesque movements, and uttering singular sounds.

Meantime the chief sits calmly smoking in the midst, and merrily grunting his inimitable song. This dance lasts about an hour, when the exertion that each one has endured makes it necessary to close. The signal is given by the presiding chief, and each dancer yelps and barks like a frightened dog; and all the voices are heard through the night-air, as the Indians retreat to their respective lodges.

20

CHAPTER XVII.

A BRAVE is not permitted to wear gray hair. It is one of the numerous duties of his wife to pluck them out as soon as they appear; and so great is their love for black hair that if, by mistake, she takes out one that is not gray, a sharp pinch reminds her of the error, and insures more care and closer observation in future. Though, as a general thing, an Indian will not work, it is said by persons who have lived among them that he usually combs his wife's or wives' hair each day.

It is a relief to find a gleam of humanity in savage nature, and their respect for the aged may be cited as one. Unlike most uncivilized people, the Indian is respectful to the aged and infirm, exceedingly careful of his sick, and patient to their wants and requirements. Despite the rugged and exposed life they lead, there are comparatively few cripples and deformed persons among them. It is said, however, that deformed infants are regarded as unprofitable and a curse from the Great Spirit, and disposed of by death immediately after their birth.   In some instances, when a daughter is born, instead of a desired son, she shares the same fate.   An instance of this came under my observation at Fort Laramie.   Sometimes, at the death of a mother, the infant is also interred.   A story to this effect is related by Mr. Boller:

"A whole family had been carried off by small-pox, except an infant.   Those who were not sick had as much to do as they could conveniently attend to, consequently there was no one willing to take charge of the little orphan.   It was placed in the arms of its dead mother, enveloped in blankets and a buffalo-robe, and laid upon a scaffold in their burying-ground.   Its cries were heard for some time, but at last they grew fainter, and finally were stilled altogether in the cold embrace of death, with the north wind sounding its requiem, and the wolves howling in the surrounding gloom — a fitting dirge for so sad a fate.   Never again would that mother and her child be separated."

There are not wanting examples of numerous noble and self-sacrificing men, who have endeavored to lead these heathen to the true light; but they have been poorly rewarded for their pains.

The plan of adopting and educating little Indian boys in the precepts of Christianity has been attempted by many of those good people, but without success.

I remember of a noble effort, near Fort Deer-Creek,

on the part of two missionaries of the Lutheran
Church, Germans by birth, who had been for several
years among the savages, striving, with worthy zeal,
to inculcate the doctrines of the apostles into their
heathen breasts, but in which they were singularly
unsuccessful. They had adopted several little boys,
who sickened and died just when their progress gave
promise of success ; and only one was left. Yet they
toiled on in the good but unrewarded labor, that
appeared, as the barren fig-tree, to yield no fruit. Perhaps their inward light showed them a clearer hope
than outward observation supplied ; and they perse-
vered, mindful of the blessed promise, " Be not weary
in well-doing, for in due time ye shall reap if ye faint
not."

The Sioux seldom leave their sick behind when they
proceed upon hunting excursions — as the families go,
that the women may dress the meat; and as they
remain away, sometimes, for months, it is an avoid-
ance of the transportation of a goodly portion of their
game. And invariably, in their migrations, the sick
and aged are taken along, regardless of the discomforts
of haste; and they always endeavor to bear away their
wounded and dead from the battle-field. If heroism
is shown in Indian life, it is when the storm of combat
gathers, and the dark cloud of war lowers over the
field of battle, striking their warriors, one after another, with the hand of death, and calling out the
noble qualities of their nature, as they fearlessly expose themselves to danger and peril to secure a fellow-

companion from the hands of an enemy, uttering the startling war-cry of defiance, as they proudly bear him from the field of slaughter or die by his side, which latter they have not anticipated until it is unavoidable, and they yield to the inevitable.

When extreme age shrivels the form, drying up the blood and palsying the muscles, they assume a mummified appearance, which is extremely repulsive — all the hair gone from the dark skull-like head, the eyebrows and eyelashes plucked out, the unsheltered and shrunken eyes apparently gone from their sockets, the whole face and neck having assumed the appearance of a mass of wrinkles, the figure very low and bent and decrepit, the withered cheeks scaled with paint, and the shrunken remains of life and animal instinct huddled together in a blanket or buffalo-robe, endeavoring to retain a spark of life that seemed to have been kindled in a mummy of a past century. The figure looks more like some distorted image of the imagination than a human being; yet, when the sound of the war-drum, and the fearful song and whoop ring through the village, aged nondescripts — such as I have attempted to describe — seem suddenly endowed with vitality, and will spring up and join in the war-dance, frantically yelling and screaming the shrill notes of the battle-song — sometimes recounting, in broken voice, the achievements of their youth.

Miserable and helpless as these octogenarians appear, they are never the less honorably and tenderly cared for. One particularly attracted attention. She

20*

had been paralyzed for a great many years, and was still the object of unremitting care—thus proving that the religious sentiment enjoined by God himself, "Honor thy father and thy mother," is inculcated by the Divine will into the savage breast as well as in our own. It is a redeeming feature in their dreary lives, and compensates for much that is harsh and cruel in their habits.

The Sioux place their dead among the branches of standing trees, if they are near timber; but when distant from any timber, upon scaffolds. The body is wrapped in a blanket or buffalo-robe; and the various things necessary for immediate comfort, such as a cup to drink from, a knife, bow, etc., are placed with the body, for the use of the spirits. The ground of a favorable place of consignment for their dead presents a revolting appearance, being strewn with parts of decaying bodies, the skulls and bones, in all stages of decomposition. By some, however, the bones are buried, after a certain length of time. The mode of burial differs in almost every tribe. The Digger Indians of California burn the body, and the friends of the deceased blacken their faces with the charred remains, and then bury the ashes. In some tribes they go through the same process, except the ashes are cast into a running stream, and carried away with the current; while, from fear lest the disembodied spirit should lurk around his former tenement, they energetically lash the air with long whips, to drive it to its spirit-home.

The Utahs bury in the clefts of rocks overlooking the cañons, and pile boulders around the body, to keep at bay the beasts of prey.   When their chief dies, his body is buried, his arms, etc., are interred with him, his horses and dogs are killed, that he may not want for anything when on his journey to the land of spirits, and a hole is left in the rocks in which he is enclosed, and food, from time to time, is in this manner placed at his disposal for several days after his sepulchre has been closed.

The Osages of Kansas observe the same rule, interring their dead among the rocks, sometimes, however, leaving them upon the ground, and covering them with earth and bark, and leaving food at the grave. If a warrior dies, his horse is killed.   If he was not in possession of a horse, a greater supply of food is left, as they believe it will require more time to go on foot to the invisible hunting-grounds.   An instance is told of a man placing food by the grave of his wife each summer for thirty years.

Thus, like the Parsees, or fire-worshippers, these northern Indians' bodies moulder away under the action of the elements.   The Sioux are much more grieved at the death of an infant than an adult — the latter, they believe, can provide for itself in the spirit-world, while the child must depend there, as well as here, upon the mercy of others.   I do not know if they believe there are servants there to attend, in such cases, or whether it is left to saints who were more advanced in years before their departure from this present existence: the latter possibly is the most probable.

Human life is sometimes sacrificed in their zeal to secure comfort for their favorites in the spirit-land. An anecdote of the kind was related by a traveller. This man was in a village, and, when passing a chief's lodge, his attention was arrested by a low wail within, when he stopped to listen. Presently a youth came out sobbing bitterly, and sat down in front of the door, covering his face and bowing his head; several Indians were walking about the place uneasily, awaiting some important event. A slight noise was made in the lodge, and soon a brave emerged from the entrance, with a gun in his hand, advancing toward the bowed youth with a look of determination upon his face, and uttering an exclamation of satisfaction, when the poor little boy sprang up with a piteous shriek and looked around: on seeing the armed warrior, his eyes rested upon him an instant, then looked toward the snow-covered mountains; and taking his seat upon the ground, he closed his eyes, as if to say his work was done, and was instantly shot through the head by the unrelenting savage.

When in war, they sometimes poison springs, thus causing great destruction among the game as well as sending death among their enemies.

One very peculiar idea, said to be cherished among Sioux Indians, is that of a thunder-bird, which they believe soars high in the air, beyond the range of human vision, carrying upon its back a lake of fresh water. When this monster is angry, it flaps its wings, causing wind and thunder; when it winks its eyes, there is lightning; and when it spreads its tail and wings, and swoops toward the earth, the lake overflows, producing rain; and in cold seasons the ground is covered with the detached icicles from its plumage. In time of drought they suppose it is absent hatching its young.

TRADITIONS.

Peruvian traditions inform us that about three centuries prior to the arrival of their Spanish conquerors, and at a period when the inhabitants of that country were still in the rudest and most barbarous state, there suddenly appeared on one of the islands of the Lake Titicaca, two persons of most surpassing beauty of form and feature, clothed in dresses of cotton, an article unknown to the people, and its whiteness looked to them strangely mysterious: they bowed themselves in reverence before the presence of these wonderful visitors, who called themselves the children of the sun, and declared that they were sent by their Beneficent Parent, who beheld with pity the miseries of the human race, to reclaim, instruct, and guide them. The persons were Manco Capac, and his wife, who was also his sister, named Mama Oello. The simple natives flocked around them to learn the import of their divine mission.

The Peruvians had been accustomed to regard the sun with superstitious reverence, and they eagerly accepted the divinity claimed by their visitors, implicitly obeying their commands, and, turning in obedience to the divine instructions issued by the children of the Ruler of the Universe, the multitude listened, believed, and obeyed. Thus instructed by the heavenly messengers, the wild, fierce warriors of Peru laid down their war-clubs, hung up their shields, and turned their glittering spears into pruning-hooks. Renouncing their roving, barbarous life, they followed their teachers to the banks of the Apurrimac, and there, upon the fertile, but uneven plain, among the lovely gardens reared by nature's own industry, laid the foundation of the city of Cuzco. Thus, from barbarity, a people was rescued by the hand of superstition. The civilization of the Peruvians was a source of wonder to the Spanish invaders, whose career of rapine and plunder obliterated the traces of the religion of a once happy people, and covered their own name with infamy.

The form of government was a patriarchal despotism, founded upon religion. The inca was not only the head of the state, but a messenger from heaven, and his commands were regarded as oracles of divinity.

The Peruvians of the most exalted rank always appeared in the presence of the inca with burdens upon their shoulders, as a token of inferiority. Force was never necessary to insure obedience to his commands.

As writing was not practised, a fringe of the borla or crown was a token of authority never disputed. The lives and property of all were at the disposal of the royal will. The royal race was sacred, and, in order to prevent contamination, the sons of Manco Capac married their own sisters. They were called children of the sun, and descendants of Pachakamac, the deity.

Indians are fatalists in the full meaning of the term, and firm believers in the presence of disembodied spirits, both good and evil. The reader of history will remember the religious character of the Mexican and South American Indian at the time of the discovery of this country.

The history of Mexico furnishes a remarkable instance of superstition, which was, no doubt, the most potent cause of the unparalleled success of Cortez and his daring followers. Montezuma had entertained a singular fatality; hence his hopeless and futile conduct upon hearing of the landing of the Spaniards in his territory. It appears that a most portentous phenomenon occurred, in the appearance of a sister of Montezuma, who had died several years previous, and was buried in a cave, in the ancient Hebrew fashion, with a great stone at the mouth of her sepulchre. The story of this supernatural event, which was firmly believed in at the time, was as follows:

"Papantzin, after her death and burial, was discovered by a little child, sitting by a fountain in the garden. Montezuma was summoned to her presence, and she addressed him to this effect: 'After I was

dead, I found myself suddenly transported to a wide
plain, which appeared to have no bounds.   In the
middle there was a road which divided into many
paths, and on one side ran a river foaming and dashing
with a dreadful sound.   I was about to plunge into
the stream and swim to the opposite bank, when suddenly appeared before me a beautiful youth, clad in a
long robe, white as snow and dazzling as the sun.
He had wings of magnificent plumage, and his forehead bore this mark.'   Here she made the sign of the
cross, by laying her two fore-fingers across each other;
'He said to me, "Stop, it is not time to pass this river."
He then led me along the banks of the stream, where
I saw heaps of skulls and human bones, and heard
the most appalling groans.

"'Presently I discovered upon the stream large
canoes with wings, filled with men in strange dresses.
They were fair in complexion and bearded, bearing
standards in their hands and helmets on their heads.
The youth said to me, "The groans you hear are from
the souls of your ancestors, who are tormented for
their crimes.   The men you see in these canoes will
conquer this empire, and introduce the knowledge of
the true God.   Thou shalt live to be a witness of this
great revolution."   Having said these things, he vanished.   I awoke to life, and removed the stone of my
sepulchre.'   Montezuma was filled with fear at this
revelation, and had it not been for the superstition, he
could, by vigorous and well-directed opposition, have
crushed the Spanish invaders, and the name of Cortez

would have been transmitted to posterity as a reckless and incompetent adventurer, who shared the fate of Cambyses and Crassus.   Instead of this, the supersti- tious monarch saw the prophecy fulfilled, and met death at the hands of his own subjects."

CHAPTER XVIII.

SECRET OF INDIAN COURAGE—SPEECH OF BLACK-HAWK—. EXECUTION OF A MANDAN CHIEF—QUESTION OF CIVIL-IZING INDIANS.

IT has always been an object among North American savages to inculcate the belief that they are among the bravest and most sagacious people upon earth. Imbued with this faith of innate supremacy, and taught rapine and murder from their infancy, can it be wondered that they frequently raise the standard of revolt, and over the vast territory of the West carry havoc and devastation? Without finance and support, no commissary, or resources whatever, chary of life, and careful of ammunition, they resort to treachery and surprise. Without baggage or hindrance they are enabled to baffle pursuit and triumphantly mock the efforts of the army to effect their punishment. Swift in their movements, and skilful in their surprises, they suddenly appear where least expected, boldly driving the stock from the Government posts and travelling caravans. They defy pursuit with their rapidity and uncertainty in movement, and shake the lance defiantly in the face of the nation. This apparent immunity from chastisement has inspired them with confidence in their power and ability,

242

and is the source of much of their daring spirit. Once let them know their own weakness and insignificance, and the war-chief would become a myth, and his deeds a story of the past. The Indian would sink into listless apathy and repose.

Black Hawk expressed in the following speech their position in his own words when he said: "I once thought I could conquer the whites; my heart grew bitter and my hand strong; I dug up the hatchet and led my warriors to battle. But the white men were mighty; I and my people have failed; I see the strength of the white man; I will be the white man's friend; I will go to my people and speak well of him; I will tell them the white men are like the leaves of the forest, very many and very strong, and that I will fight no more against them."

Thus it is their ignorance and vanity that causes much of their futile effort to turn back the march of empire. They strengthen their faith by unbelief and incredulity, refusing to hear testimony of the whites and even of their own people to whom have been given opportunities to ascertain by observation the strength of their enemies. The fate of the Mandan chief illustrates the extent of their prejudices, and the confidence with which they regard their own power.

In the year 1822, Major O. Fallon attended a delegation of the principal chiefs to Washington — warriors from the Kansas, Pawnees, Ottoes, Gros Ventres, Mandans, Omahaws, and other tribes. For the purpose of showing them the futility of resistance to such strength and power, these chiefs were taken to Washington, Baltimore, Philadelphia, and New York. They took careful note of everything; they measured the length of the vessels by pacing the decks; measured the guns of the forts with strings; also took the length of some of the public buildings, etc.; and even attempted to count the people of New York city, and keep a record of their number upon notched sticks.

On their return they ventured to give an account of what they had seen: in every instance this was received with incredulity, and in most cases it was fatal to the chiefs' reputation for veracity. The fate of the Mandan chief was melancholy: upon his return he ventured to give without exaggeration what he had seen: "The white people," said he, "have lodges some of which are a hundred paces in length; they have canoes fifty paces long, and they will convey safely five hundred men; the people of the great villages are as numerous as the stars in the sky, or the straws on the prairie." This announcement they received with universal disbelief: some of them rose up in council and told the chief it could not be true, that he had sought to deceive them, and spoken with a double tongue. In vain he protested that he told the truth; in vain did he appeal to the Great Spirit in attestation of his veracity. "You have spoken falsely," they cried; "you shall die." However they may practise deceptions on an enemy, they strictly adhere to the truth among themselves: an attempt to practise deceit upon the tribe is held to be an unworthy act, degrading to a warrior, and a foul sin against the Great Spirit; it is considered that a man had better die, and thus put an end to sinning, than live defiled by falsehood.

Proceeding upon this belief, the Mandan savages were called out for the execution of their chief, whom they had in public council pronounced a liar. " Sing your death-song," they said; and the brave chief, knowing their ignorance and custom, sang the death-chant, and declared his readiness to die. Several Indians then fired, and the soul of the chief that had dared to tell the truth passed on to the hunting-lands of his fathers. Thus, among savages as among the most enlightened people, ignorance is ever bigoted. Galileo was persecuted for asserting that the earth revolved; Socrates condemned for declaring the truth; and the Mandan chief executed because he asserted that the white man had canoes fifty paces in length.

The Indians that have come mostly under my observation are Sioux and Cheyennes, together with the Omahaws, Gros Ventres, Pawnees, Delawares, Shawnees, Osages, and Kansas, and others that are settled along the borders or on reserves, amid the industrious settlers of that thrifty State. In conclusion, I can but say Indians in one tribe are much like those in another, bearing a marked resemblance in habits and customs. In courage they do not equal the white man, notwithstanding all that has been written to the contrary; while their conceptions of policy are narrow and selfish. The Indian of to-day is not one step in advance of his ancestry of centuries

21 *

ago ; and the intelligent American must blush for the contaminating influence of his race, when he beholds the copy of the worst sins that degrade the white man exhibited by the ignorant Indian, to whom his superior brother has been apparently a missionary of evil.

Perhaps the possibility of civilizing the savage may be questioned. I remember visiting a Shawnee village during Christmas holidays. These Indians are considered civilized, and their villages boast of schools, churches, and all the institutions of a refined and enlightened community. Many white people reside there. At that time, I remember most disgraceful scenes on New Year and Christmas days, when large groups of squaws, violently and furiously excited with spirituous liquor, ran through the streets, blaspheming in a most shocking manner, and exhibiting traits of character too brutish to be expected even from their savage nature.

Two years later, being overtaken by a storm while visiting some friends in Kansas, in company with two brothers, I sought shelter in a vacated house in an Indian village belonging to the Sac and Fox reservation, which, though well built and commodious, had been deserted. Its roof, too, had been torn off, to furnish tent-poles for a summer residence. In the floor holes had been cut, through which to sink the legs of the bedsteads ; and in a like manner everything betrayed a desire to return to their primitive habits, from which an attempt had been made by Government to withdraw them. Substantial buildings of stone had been erected for them, dotting their reservation, but they had put up their lodges by the side of the houses, and stabled their horses within the nicely plastered rooms. With a view to the artistic, they had ornamented the white walls with designs and figures representing scalping performances, big Indians on horseback, and big Indians on foot, until the walls resembled a badly damaged map of the physical geography of the United States, with the aborigines, mammoth bison, and in short all the mammalia of the country in mortal combat.

Rev. G. W. Freeman gives an interesting account of an effort, on the part of the Government, to civilize the Pawnees. These Indians inhabit a country bordering on the Platte River, who were once a powerful tribe, but a state of continual war with the Sioux has diminished them to a comparatively small tribe. By request of the agent, Major Troath, Mr. Freeman visited the reserve, situated upon the Loup Fork, about twenty-three miles from Columbus, Nebraska, and found it occupying the site of the old Mormon village, Genoa. This mission was located in the year 1857, the grounds being fifteen by thirty miles in extent, and, according to a recent census, contains two thousand four hundred and one souls. They receive sixty thousand dollars per year, and this is divided between the school and the business interests of the tribe. They engage in agriculture, and practical men are employed to instruct them in the mechanical arts. The school is under the charge of Mrs. Platte and two assistants. The branches taught are reading, orthography, geography, arithmetic, analysis, and penmanship.

Mr. Freeman says that many of the present pupils have been in the school from two to four years, and have attained, to some degree, a knowledge of the English language, and the rudiments of education; but when not in school they immediately return to their native language and Indian songs, refusing to speak the English dialect, except when in the presence of their teachers, when it is spoken for praise, as they are extremely fond of flattery. They are addicted to falsehood and theft. It is the opinion of the Rev. Mr. Freeman that these Indians will eventually abandon the apparel of civilization, and relapse into their original wild costumes and habits. It is also his impression that unless these pupils are kept entirely away from the wild tribes, where the influence of religion and morality is not felt, all benefits from civilizing them will prove futile.

It is melancholy indeed, to review the history of the North American Indian, from the days of Cortez and Pizarro until the present moment. The aborigines of this country are fast disappearing — not becoming lost in the people by marriage and intermixture, but by the hand of death. Like the buffalo upon which they subsist, the day is not far distant when their virtues and their crimes will be as a tale that is told — a legend over which the future historian will ponder, and the artist draw imaginary portraitures.

CONCLUSION.

IN April, 1865, after a residence of eight months in Fort Laramie, my husband's health being re-established, he determined to proceed to Denver City, in Colorado. In taking leave of Fort Laramie and our many new friends, kind feelings rose in our breasts for those whose consideration and politeness toward us during our stay had endeared them to memory in the future. Our intention of crossing the country to Colorado became known in the neighboring Indian village some time before we started, and a tragical ending came nigh being effected.

The Indians were considered hostile all over the country, from the border of Kansas to Utah Territory; yet a few still lingered around the fort, who were considered friendly; but, as the Indians of the hills were always cognizant of the military proceedings at the fort, their loyalty might be doubted.

Soon after our arrival at Fort Laramie, twelve chiefs had visited us. Two days previous to the day appointed for our departure, a squad of soldiers left Fort Laramie en route for Colorado, and, believing it safer to go with soldiers, we hastily made our preparations, and started with them. Our journey was attended with no misfortune; but, on the day we had expected to go, a party of mountaineers, with whom we had intended travelling, set out. When they stopped for dinner they were surprised by a large body of savages, who surrounded the train and commenced a vigorous search of the wagons, using harsh measures and threatening violence to the travellers, who were indignant at the unexpected attack; for they were known to be friends to the Indians.

Among the company was a German family, that had resided near Fort Laramie for several years, and, having been very kind to the Indians, were held in great respect by the various bands of the country, one of which had adopted the lady into their tribe, giving her the name of White Sister, and to her they communicated the object of the search, and expressed their revengeful feelings toward us. At length, becoming convinced that we were not of the company, they took their departure in a disappointed and ferocious manner; not, however, until they had received a large number of presents.

As the angry braves dashed off, Mrs. Forbes, the lady that was called White Sister, communicated to the astonished company the object of the search.

On our journey to Denver, we stopped a few weeks at Camp Collins, a military station on the Cachelapoudre River. This fort was commanded by Captain Evans, who received us kindly. It was our first acquaintance with any persons of that place.

Soon after our arrival, General Moonlight arrived, being en route to Fort Laramie, to take command of that district. Having been acquainted with my husband when he was in the military service, and believing Fort Laramie would be a good place for him, he urged us to return and resume business. Having concluded, however, to go to Denver City, we declined the kind invitation.

While at Camp Collins we heard of the death of President Lincoln, and, although separated by distance from the immediate interests of the great struggle, we joined in the mournful honors of the time.

After arriving in Denver, we immediately engaged in business; but not liking that city as a place for our home, we soon left it; yet during the succeeding years our home has been in the far West, and our interests and affections centre among its people.

Having frequently been solicited to narrate our experiences with the Indians in the order of their occurrence, after the lapse of more than five years I have endeavored to recount them in a plain and unadorned manner, together with a few other instances of life among the Sioux, and some historical facts of that people.

All that is not the result of personal observation has been gleaned from reliable sources.

In conclusion, I present this little volume to the public, asking kindly consideration for its errors, and trusting that any deficiency in brilliancy may be excused in so unpretending a recital.

My unfortunate friend, Mrs. Kelley, whom I left in the Indian camp when I escaped with my child,

remained with those Indians four months, suffering
all the privations and hardships of a white slave with
a roving band of hostile savages.   At the expiration
of that time, she was taken by the Blackfeet Sioux,
and remained with them some time, but was finally
ransomed at Fort Sully.   For want of space in this
volume, which is already larger than was originally
intended, I am compelled to omit the particulars of
her sufferings, privations and ransom, but give them,
as related by herself, in a book entitled "Mrs. Kelley's
Experience among the Indians."

THE END.

www.ingramcontent.com/pod-product-compliance
Lightning Source LLC
Chambersburg PA
CBHW031418020726
47499CB00005B/1493